The Elusive Beaches Of Eleuthera

2007 Edition

by

Geoff and Vicky Wells

Geezer Guides
(div. of DataIsland Software LLC)
Hollywood Florida USA

The Elusive Beaches Of Eleuthera ~ 2007 Edition

International Standard Book Number: 0-9772346-0-6

Library of Congress Control Number: 2006906699

Printed and bound in Canada

First Printing: December 2006

00 09 08 07 06

The Elusive Beaches of Eleuthera ~ 2007 Edition

Geoff and Vicky Wells

DataIsland Software

3389 Sheridan Street #521

Hollywood, Florida

33021

Tel.: (866) 228-5312

e-mail: beachologists@elusivebeaches.com

Website: www.elusivebeaches.com

Mr. Ivan Ferguson, J.P.
Administrator - Central Eleuthera District
Governor's Harbour, Eleuthera, Bahamas

Perched on the northeastern edge of the great Bahama Bank approximately 370 km east of Miami, is Eleuthera, one of the gems of The Bahamian archipelago.

Geoff and Vicky Wells capture the essence of spectacular beaches and rare landmarks in their book, 'The Elusive Beaches of Eleuthera'.

The enchantment surrounding the pristine beaches of Eleuthera is legendary. The explicit directions, facilitated by global positioning, unearth indigenous landmarks on the Isle of Freedom. As a result, visitors and local residents have the benefit of easy access to historic sites and commercial establishments.

'The Elusive Beaches of Eleuthera' encapsulates and unveils some unique phenomena of unspoilt beauty which peaks readers' interests.

Ivan Ferguson

Beach•ol•o•gy |bē CH äləjē|

noun

the study of the composition, attractiveness, and location of sandy areas adjacent to oceans.

• the study of comparative population density on sandy areas.

DERIVATIVES

beachological |bē CH ōˈläjikəl| adjective

beachologically |bē CH ōˈläjik(ə)lē| adverb

beachologist |-jist| noun

ORIGIN late 20th cent.: from "The Elusive Beaches of Eleuthera" (see **http://www.elusivebeaches.com**).

When we coined the term "Beachologists" as a fun way to describe what we do we had no idea it would actually enter the language and be used by other people. Google now returns over 200 hits and since we can't see any listings prior to our book's release we think it is fair to claim the credit for this new "science".

We wrote the first edition almost seven years ago and we are delighted our little book has become so popular. It has sold thousands of copies, been the subject of numerous discussions on Eleuthera bulletin boards and recommended by The Lonely Planet Guide.

We want to thank all of you for buying the book and the kind words and encouragement we have received from your e-mails. We hope you enjoy our new web site http://www.elusivebeaches.com and that you will stop by and leave your comments or upload your best Eleuthera photos.

The beaches of Eleuthera are fabulous. Much of the shoreline is beach but unfortunately access to these beaches is limited. Because there is very little commercial development there is no one to clean the beaches or to maintain access roads. The access roads (if you can call them that) are generally just tracks through the bush cut by local farmers to get to their crops. Sometimes the roads are part of a subdivision and may be paved but even these are often overgrown. There are no "To the Beach" signs and no guarantees that roads you take will go anywhere near a beach.

The Elusive Beaches of Eleuthera is designed to change all that. We give you explicit directions and distances from local landmarks to accessible beaches plus warnings about road conditions and the type of vehicle you will need to travel them. We provide GPS (Global Positioning Satellite) readings for each turn you make off the Queen's Highway and where each access road meets the beach.

The majority of accessible beaches are located towards the northern end of the island where there is slightly more population. However, there are many fine beaches at the southern end of the island and we hope you will make the effort to check them out.

We have personally inspected each beach and rated each one in several useful categories. We hope you agree with our assessments but would appreciate any comments you have on our ratings.

The Ratings

We rate each beach in several different categories. The average rating is three with any special considerations, good or bad, affecting the rating up or down. Each of the listings in *The Elusive Beaches of Eleuthera* displays a series of five colored icons. If the first icon is circled, the beach has only scored a one. If the third icon is circled, the beach has scored a three, and so on. You get the idea.

The Beaches

A beach which scores three is a nice place to spend the day. Nothing out of the ordinary, just average. If it scores one it is just a place that provides access to the water. It may have other redeeming features such as being a good shelling beach but don't plan to spend your vacation here. Beaches we have given a five rating are rare and very special places. These are the ones you see in the travel brochures. They provide a perfect combination of sun, surf, sand and shade. Lighthouse beach at the southern most tip of Eleuthera is just such a place. In our opinion it is the best beach on the island. It has miles of flat, cool pink sand, shallow calm waters, a high degree of privacy and a cave for shelter from the afternoon sun. We rate each of the other beaches against this standard. The Atlantic beaches tend to be wide and the water gets deep fairly quickly. There is generally significant wave action and some undertow. The sand may be covered in a fair bit of flotsam, which is great for beachcombing. On the Caribbean side waves are rare and at many sites you can wade out hundreds of feet and still touch the bottom. Shelling is possible at sites on both sides but we think that on the Caribbean side you are more likely to find the best, unbroken specimens. The Queen's Highway is mostly on the Caribbean side so these beaches are the easiest to get to but there are fewer than on the Atlantic side.

Directions

There are very few road name signs and almost nothing in the way of landmarks that we can use in the directions. In order to properly direct you to each site we have decided to use two methods. First and most accurate we have taken GPS readings at each turning and at each beach access. Hand held units are readily available and will provide you with absolute assurance that you are on the right track. We also give you the distance in miles and kilometers from prominent businesses that are easily found along the highway. We tell you the length of each access road so you don't get discouraged and turn back when a magnificent beach is just around the next bend.

We refer to the Atlantic or Caribbean side for convenience and to indicate the character of the water. We are well aware that Eleuthera is not technically in the Caribbean and each end of the island is not really in the Atlantic.

Access

The condition of beach access roads and the type of vehicle you will need to negotiate them varies considerably. Many of Eleuthera's beaches can be visited in a regular sedan. Paved, or at least smooth, roads go to a good selection of excellent beaches. To get to the very best that Eleuthera has to offer you will need an SUV with good ground clearance. It's unlikely that you will need to engage the 4-wheel drive but it is comforting to know that it is available. A five rating means paved road all the way, a one rating means you need to rent a tank.

Privacy

There are lots of beaches and very few people. Many of the best beaches require an effort to reach them so there is a good chance that you will have the beach to yourselves. Sometimes this means miles of pink sand with no one but you and your mate. If you are tempted to skinny dip be warned that public nudity is an offence in the Bahamas. The key word here is "public" and whether a secluded beach can be considered such. The actual wording of the law from "The Statute Law of The Bahamas Islands, Volume II" - Waterlow & Sons Limited, London, England 1965, reads,

Penal Code, Chapter 48 Section 230 (12)

"Every person who does any of the following acts shall, in every case be liable to a penalty of twenty pounds, ($100.00) that is to say, every person who:-

(12) willfully and indecently exposes his person in any public place or within view thereof, or in any place with intent to insult any female"

Penal Code, Chapter 48 Section 529

"Whoever publicly and willfully commits any grossly indecent act is guilty of a misdemeanor."

Any fine would be discretionary.

We leave the interpretation up to you. We will however rate each beach by the amount of privacy you can expect. Note that a rating of five does not guarantee absolute privacy, after all, you found it...

Swimming

With huge expanses of warm water at a relatively constant depth and smooth white sand bottom the Caribbean side offers the best swimming. Atlantic beaches are characterized by the large waves found at "Surfer's Beach" in Gregory Town. The constant pounding of Atlantic waves has created the best beaches and several bays at each end of Eleuthera are sheltered by reefs which produces conditions similar to the Caribbean. Of course there are exceptions to these generalities so read the listings carefully.

Snorkeling

The "Ocean Hole", "Sweeting's Pond" and the small cove beside "Hidden Beach" are the only areas in our book we would consider true "dive" sites. Many beaches have interesting snorkeling areas and most are in shallow water. On the Atlantic side several bays are protected by long reefs but these should only be visited in a boat and we have not included them in our ratings.

Beachcombing

In general the beaches on the Caribbean side have the best selection of intact shells. If your beachcombing search is for other items then the Atlantic beaches will yield rope, nets, buoys, buckets and driftwood in an endless variety.

Supplies

You're likely used to finding a gas station on every corner and a fast food joint any time you're hungry. Fortunately Eleuthera is not that well developed so you should plan accordingly. Make sure your gas tank is full and take bottled water and sunscreen. It is easy to get dehydrated playing on the beach. Most of all have a great time, come back often and enjoy *The Elusive Beaches of Eleuthera.*

Geoff & Vicky Wells, DB (Doctors of Beachology)

Hatchet Bay

Eleuthera

beachologists@elusivebeaches.com

Contents

* whenever possible we provide the local name for a beach but sometimes beaches are unnamed or we cannot find one. In these cases we have named them ourselves.

Harbour Island

N 25° 29.500' ~ W 76° 38.000'

The miles-long pink sand beach on Harbour Island is probably the most well known beach in Eleuthera and perhaps the most photographed as well. It has been featured in many travel magazines and articles not only for the spectacular beach but also because of the number of celebrities that frequent the island. The reef-protected beach is wide and the water is shallow and calm even though it is on the Atlantic side. All the expensive hotels here keep the beach well cleaned and groomed. The rest of Eleuthera's beaches are "au naturel".

Directions to access road

2.5 miles (4.0 kms) east of **North Eleuthera Texaco** along the road that passes North Eleuthera airport. This road ends at the dock where you can board a water taxi to Harbour Island. Water taxis run frequently and will set out when they have enough passengers. Don't worry if you miss one, there'll be another along in mere moments.

Leave the highway at the ferry dock

Once you take the ferry over to Harbour Island you can walk to the beach or rent a golf cart. We'd suggest a golf cart as there's lots to explore on this island besides the beach. Just be careful on some of the roads and be sure to respect people's property. Take your time exploring this beautiful island.

Access

The highway runs all the way to the water taxi dock and there is plenty of parking space. The fare to Harbour Island is currently $4 per person each way and boats come and go all day.

Privacy

Most of the resorts are situated along this beautiful beach. Don't expect any privacy at all. But it's still a perfect setting for a long, romantic stroll on the beach, or a quick splash in the gentle waves.

Swimming

As the water remains calm and the bottom is even and sandy, this is a great place for sunning, swimming and people watching. So go ahead, frolic in the water, swim, paddle or just splash around.

Snorkeling

Check with some of the locals for the best snorkeling spots around the island. We're sure you'll get lots of differing opinions and find people willing to point you in the right direction. Also, check out the local dive operators.

Beachcombing

We didn't find a lot of shells on this beach. The beach gets cleaned on a regular basis and with it also being reef protected not a lot of shells get left on the beach. But while you're strolling along the beach, keep your eyes open. You never know what you might find.

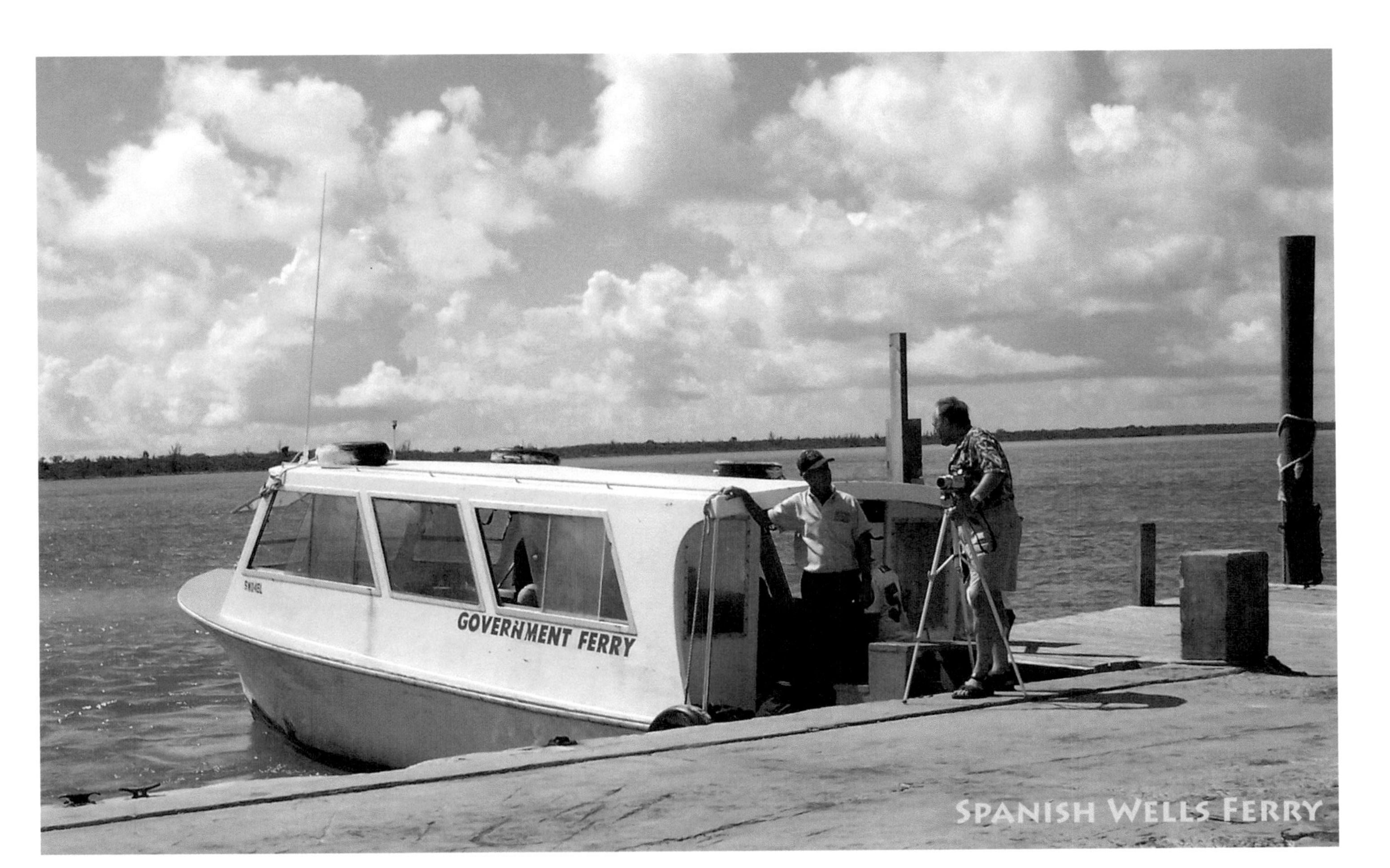

Spanish Wells Ferry

N 25° 32.725' ~ W 76° 45.208'

The settlement of Spanish Wells is bordered on two sides by some fabulous beach. The sand is white, soft and powdery. Just right for a long stroll. The water is shallow for a good distance out. This is a great place to bring small children to play in the water. Although we've heard people say that they didn't find the residents of Spanish Wells to be very friendly, we have never experience that. Anyone we have spoken with has been welcoming and helpful. While you're there, take the time to listen the residents unique accent. It's simply a joy to hear.

Directions to access road

6.5 miles (10.5 kms) north of **North Eleuthera Texaco** is the ferry dock. You'll want to take the part of the highway that passes Builders Square not the Scotia Bank (if you pass Scotia Bank you're on the road to North Eleuthera airport). You can catch a water taxi at the dock to take you to Spanish Wells.

Leave the highway at the ferry dock

Take the ferry from Gene's Bay to this settlement and then rent a golf cart or just walk to the beach. If you head directly across the island from the ferry dock you'll run right into the beach.

Access

The highway runs all the way to the water taxi dock and there is plenty of parking space. The return fare to Spanish Wells is currently $5 per person but is subject to change without notice. Recently, they have started giving out tokens for your return trip.

Privacy

There are houses all along the beach. You won't find any privacy here. But don't let that stop you from enjoying the warm, turquoise water, soft white sand and gently lapping waves.

Swimming

The water is calm and shallow almost all the time. Wade in and go for a swim. Or, just immerse yourself in the sun-warmed, amazingly clear water. If you've walked here you'll want to cool off a bit anyway.

Snorkeling

While walking the beach we had a few small fish darting around our ankles. Give snorkeling a try and you'll get a better look at all the colorful fish. You may have to walk a little ways out for the water to get even deep enough to snorkel.

Beachcombing

We found some terrific, intact, shells while walking this beach. Even clam-type shells with both sides still attached. Most of them were small, but because this beach is so shallow the waves never get very rough and a lot of shells remain pristine.

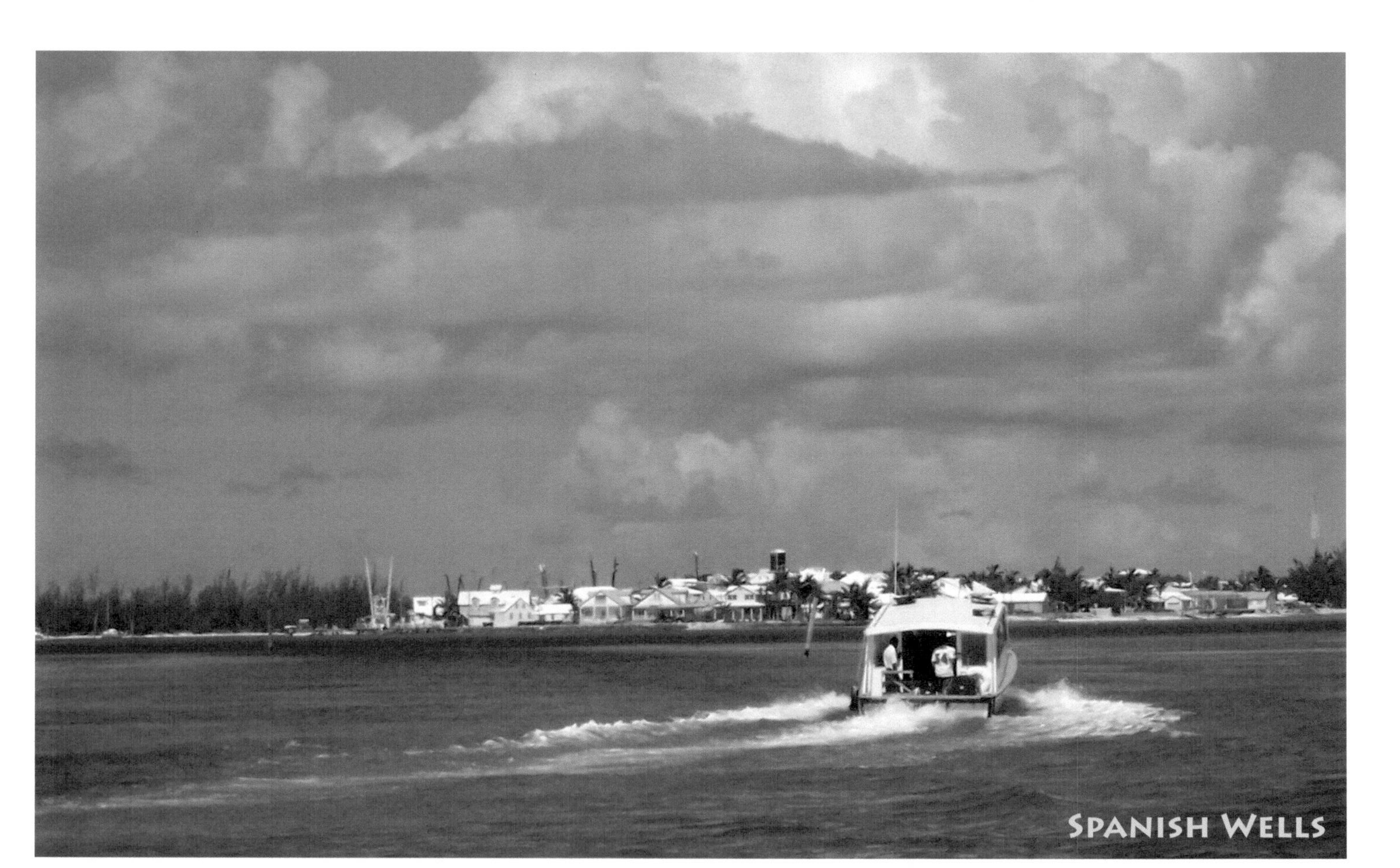

Spanish Wells

Salt Kettle Bay Beach

N 25° 33.449'~W 76° 44.097'

REVISED: Often referred to as Ridley Head (which is the rocky point at the beginning of this bay), this popular beach has soft, cool, pink, powdery sand and is quite wide. The firmly packed sand makes it a good beach for those long, leisurely strolls. We are sorry to report that, since the last edition of this book, access to Salt Kettle Bay Beach, by road, has been restricted. There is a barrier across the access road declaring it as Private Property. And, as always, we encourage you to respect private property.

Directions to access road

Go north from **North Eleuthera Texaco** towards Spanish Wells. Take the 90 degree bend to the left and go a total of 6.1 miles (9.8 kms) to the dirt road on your right. This is the second road past the bend and the last road before the ferry dock at Gene's Bay.

Leave the highway at N 25° 32.966'~W 76° 43.615'

and follow the road without making any turns for 1.0 miles (1.7 kms) passing through a small village. At a fork in the road is where you will encounter a chain barrier and the Private Property sign. We always encourage you to respect other's property. So, if you have access to a boat, you can always use the GPS coordinates to get to the beach by boat.

Access

With a little caution over the bumpy areas, this beach can be accessed by any car. There are a couple of spots where you'll need to go very slowly. But remember, access across private property is now restricted. You won't be able to drive to the beach.

Privacy

This is a fairly well-known beach and we encountered people that came in by car and by boat. As road access is now restricted, you'll need a boat to visit this beach. Don't expect much privacy here.

Swimming

Even though this beach is on the Atlantic side, the water is fairly calm most of the time. The bottom is sandy and even but becomes quite deep on a gradual slope. If you're going by boat, it would be best to go on a calm day.

Snorkeling

You can try snorkeling around some of the rocky areas and you might be pleasantly surprised. But just to be safe, always be sure to confine both swimming and snorkeling to calm days.

Beachcombing

We didn't find a lot of shells on this beach and what shells there were were scattered and uninteresting. But as we always suggest, keep your eyes open. You just never know.

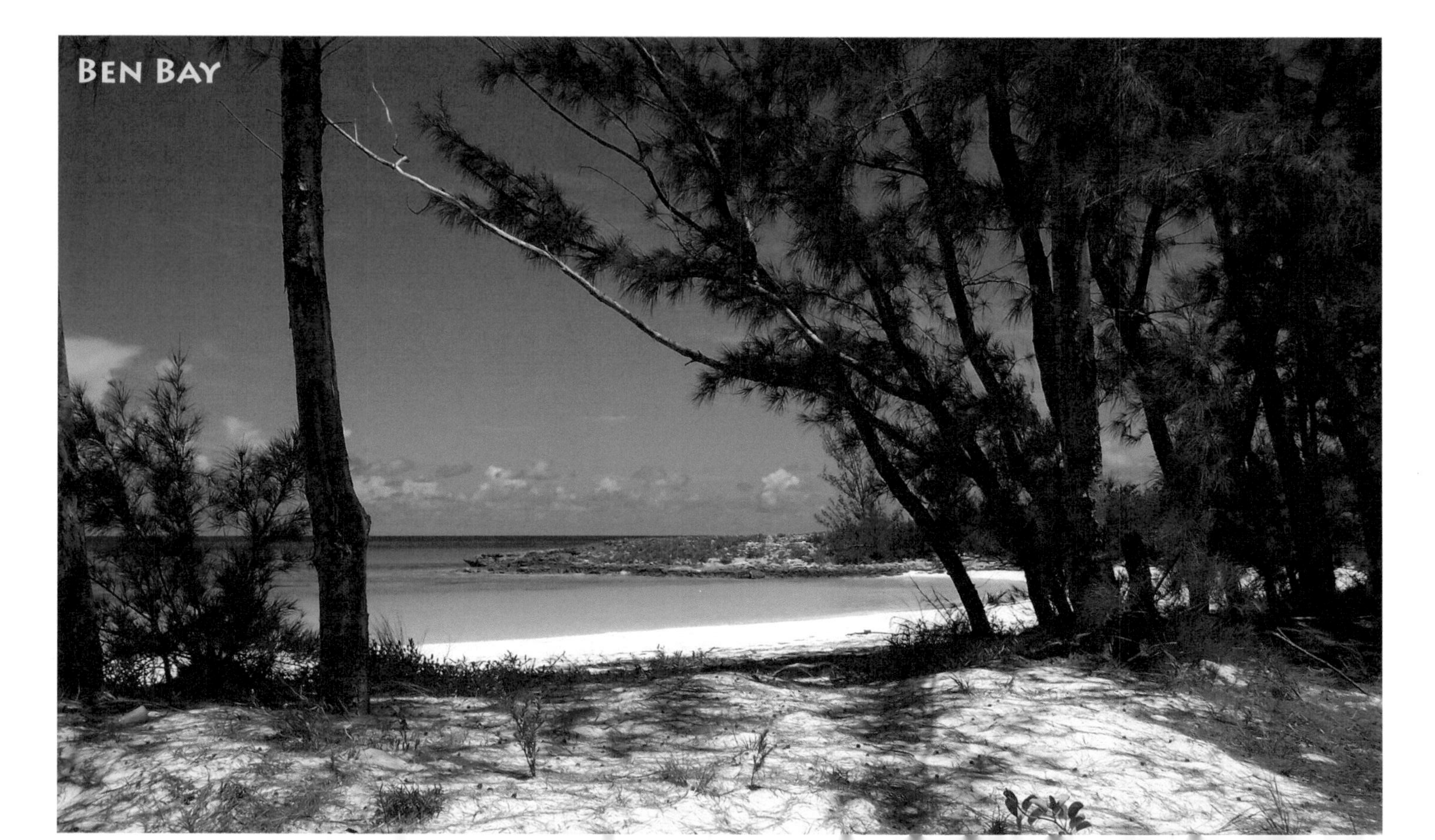
BEN BAY

N 25° 33.501'~W 76° 43.417'

REVISED: This horseshoe-shaped beach is like something you'd find on a postcard. It simply couldn't be more perfect. The narrow opening to the bay provides a lot of protection for the beach and even when the Atlantic is rough the water in the bay stays calm. Without proper directions this must-see beach would be almost impossible to find but with the directions below it's easy.

Directions to access road

Go north from **North Eleuthera Texaco** towards Spanish Wells. Take the 90 degree bend to the left and go a total of 6.0 miles (9.7 kms) to the dirt road on your right. This is the first road past the bend and the second to last road before the ferry dock at Gene's Bay.

Leave the highway at N 25° 32.992'~W 76° 43.565'

and go for a total of 0.75 miles (1.2 kms) making the following turns: at 0.2 miles (0.35 kms) take the fork to the left; at 0.3 miles (0.55 kms) take the fork to the right (the road to the left looks like better road but be sure to go right); at 0.5 miles (0.85 kms) turn left. It gets pretty overgrown at this point, so don't get discouraged. Stay on this road right to the beach. Also note that, as of this printing, on your right will be a cleared field. In the previous edition this was all overgrown as well.

Access

Although the access road is flat and even, it's overgrown in several places. You get a scenic tour past some fields growing citrus fruits, bananas and papayas on your way to the beach. Please no sampling this is someone's livelihood.

Privacy

There are no houses and no other roads into this beach. Odds are you'll have it all to yourselves. We've been there a number of times and never seen anyone else. However, there has frequently been evidence that there were others there before us.

Swimming

The swimming here is great. We didn't want to leave. The water is clear and calm, the bottom is sandy and even. It can get a bit deep in the middle of the bay, but it usually wasn't over our heads.

Snorkeling

Be sure to bring your snorkel gear along. You can stay inside the bay and snorkel the rocky areas that protect the beach. Be sure to pick a calm day, though. This is the Atlantic side after all.

Beachcombing

As with most areas that are so well protected from the waves, the shells don't get through either. We found a few very small ones but had to really look for those. But we did get a photo op with a rather territorial sand crab.

Preacher's Cave

N25° 33.439' ~ W76° 41.768'

NEW: Preacher's Cave is not only a natural formation that's worth seeing, it also has historical significance. When the Eleutherian Adventurers were shipwrecked on the Devil's Backbone in the mid-1700s, they sought refuge in this cave. Religious services have been held at this site, on and off, since that time. Be sure to read the plaque at the entrance and walk right inside to get a feel for the size and to get a look at the natural "skylights".

Directions to access road

5.7 miles (9.2 kms) north of **North Eleuthera Texaco** turn right onto a gravel road. Watch for the sign pointing to Preacher's Cave. The larger sign has been restored, making it easier to find your turn, but signs come and go and this larger sign has gone missing before, so be sure to follow the directions.

Leave the highway at N 25° 33.089'~W 76° 43.306'

and continue for 1.7 miles (2.7 kms) to a dirt road on your left. There's a tiny sign at this dirt road that reads "Preacher's Cave" and "Beach", so keep your eye on the mile-age because this sign can be very easy to miss. Follow this dirt road for 0.25 miles (0.4 kms). The sandy path to your right goes to the beach, the grassy path to your left goes to Preacher's Cave.

Access

This road can be a bit rough in spots, mostly on the hills where the rain has eroded the softer material. With reasonable care you can make it in a regular car. But go slow so you can see the dips and bumps - and - so you won't miss the road to Preacher's Cave.

N 25° 33.522'~W 76° 41.758'

Just opposite Preacher's Cave, this beach is long and wide with powdery soft sand. To your left, facing the water, you'll notice a rocky point. You can climb over this point to find two other, smaller beaches. To your right, walk down past a rocky outcropping and find a wonderful swimming area in a small cove created by the outcropping and another point. Spend some time here to explore not only the beach and attached "mini" beaches, but to visit Preacher's Cave as well.

Directions to access road

5.7 miles (9.2 kms) north of **North Eleuthera Texaco** turn right onto a gravel road. Watch for the sign pointing to Preacher's Cave. The larger sign has been restored, making it easier to find your turn, but signs come and go and this larger sign has gone missing before, so be sure to follow the directions.

Leave the highway at N 25° 33.089'~W 76° 43.306'

and continue for 1.7 miles (2.7 kms) to a dirt road on your left. There's a tiny sign at this dirt road that reads "Preacher's Cave" and "Beach", so keep your eye on the mileage because this sign can be very easy to miss. Follow this dirt road for 0.25 miles (0.4 kms). At the end, the sandy path to your right goes to the beach, the grassy path to your left goes to Preacher's Cave.

Access

This road can be a bit rough in spots, mostly on the hills where the rain has eroded the softer material. With reasonable care you can make it in a regular car. But go slow so you can see the dips and bumps - and - so you won't miss the road to the beach.

Privacy

As Preacher's Cave is a well known, if not easy to find, tourist attraction, you shouldn't expect much privacy at the beach just opposite this cave. You'll frequently see boaters here, too.

Swimming

The swimming at this beach is pretty good everywhere but we preferred the small cove described above. We have also been told that a trio of dolphins swam in to visit with a family swimming at this beach. We keep hoping that will happen to us.

Snorkeling

While swimming here a small ray joined us. Again, it was while we were in the small cove. It's encounters like this that make a day at the beach even more special. Please be sure to respect the wildlife, both in the water and on land.

Beachcombing

Unfortunately we didn't find many shells at all. If you look around you can find a few small ones, but nothing worth taking home.

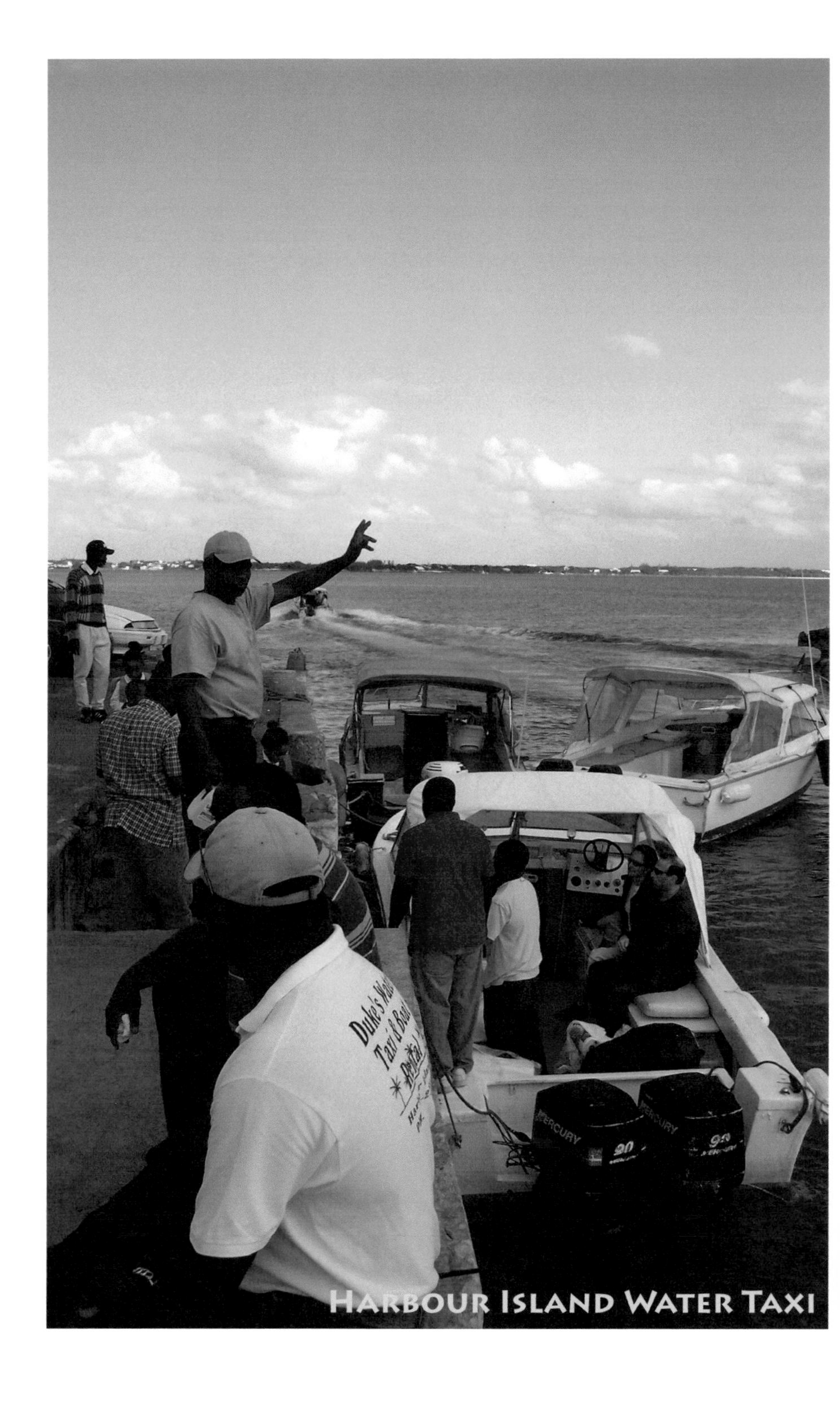

HARBOUR ISLAND WATER TAXI

Current Bay Beach

N 25° 33.395'~W 76° 41.247'

Don't let the name of this beach confuse you. It's not anywhere near the settlement of Current (see the next few pages for beaches in Current). This beach is actually in the northern part of Eleuthera. This powdery soft, multi-coved beach is a little off the beaten track but well worth the effort to find. As Current Bay Beach is just a little past the road to Preacher's Cave, you could spend time at both beaches and see Preacher's Cave all on the same day. There are palm trees and pine trees for shade making it a lovely spot to bring a picnic lunch.

Directions to access road

5.7 miles (9.2 kms) north of **North Eleuthera Texaco** turn right onto a gravel road. There is a sign at this road pointing the way to Preacher's Cave (see the Tay Bay directions).

Leave the highway at N 25° 33.089'~W 76° 43.306'

and continue for 2.3 miles (3.75 kms) to this fabulous beach. At 1.7 miles (2.7 kms) you'll pass the road to Preacher's Cave/Tay Bay. At 2.1 miles (3.4 kms) turn left onto a dirt track leading between some fenced fields. At 2.2 miles (3.55 kms) the path to the beach is on your right between some pine trees. Just pull your car off to the side and walk the rest of the way to the beach.

Access

There are a couple of rough spots along this access road, but with reasonable care any car can make it but the more clearance you have the better. Drive slowly so you can see the dips and bumps.

Privacy

Chances are, if you take the effort to find this beach, you'll have it all to yourself. But, it can be a popular spot for boaters, either anchoring to enjoy the beach, or just passing by on their way to or from Harbour Island, so don't expect a lot of privacy here.

Swimming

You can see waves breaking on a reef well offshore. This helps the water along the shoreline stay relatively calm and clean – perfect for swimming or just bobbing in the gentle waves and enjoying the warm ocean water. Always pick a calm day to visit.

Snorkeling

We didn't find a lot of areas along this beach for snorkeling but, if you've got your equipment with you anyway, you might want to give it a try. And, as we always caution, pick a calm day. The waves can kick up depending on the weather.

Beachcombing

Like most beaches that are reef protected, there aren't many shells to speak of. We did find the odd one but they were very small and scattered.

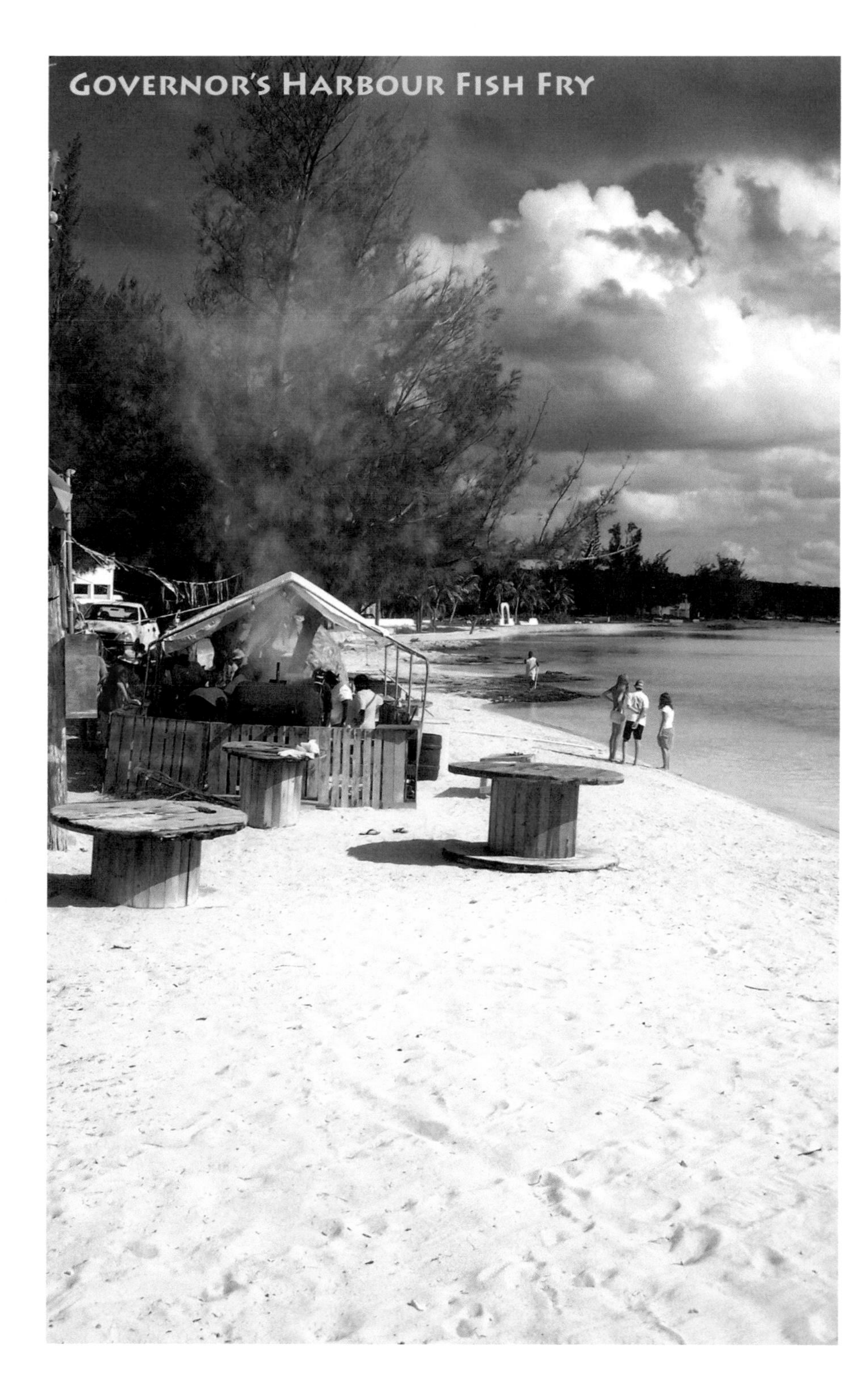

Governor's Harbour Fish Fry

Upper Cove Beach

N 25° 25.231'~W 76° 46.228'

REVISED: This sandy cove is right at Queen's Hwy on the way to the settlement of Current. The clear turquoise water is shallow and the sand is cool, pink and powdery. This will be the first beach you'll encountered on your way to the Current settlement. So if you just can't wait any longer to get in the water, stop here and enjoy.

Directions to Current

Coming from **The Cove** - at 10 miles (16.1 kms) turn left at T-junction and right at next T-junction. This puts you on the road to Current. Look for signs to the settlement of Current.

Directions to access road - heading south (from Current)

0.4 mile (0.64 kms) from **Welcome To Current** sign. From Current and heading back towards the main part of Eleuthera.

Directions to access road - heading north

14.7 miles (23.6 kms) north of **The Cove**. Follow the directions above.

Leave the highway at N 25° 25.228'~W 76° 46.222'

This small cove is right on Queen's Highway, so there is no actual access road. Just pull off to the side and enjoy the beach.

Access

This beach is easily accessible by any car as it is directly off Queen's Highway. This makes it easy to spot and easy to get to. Not all that "elusive", but certainly worth stopping by for a look.

Privacy

Don't expect any privacy here. Even though we didn't see any other footprints, the beach is visible from the highway. You may get the beach all to yourself, but be sure to wave to the passing motorists.

Swimming

This spot is a good place to go swimming. The bottom is even and sandy and the water is calm most of the time. It's not a large area, so probably just wading or bobbing in the water would be easier than trying to do any real swimming.

Snorkeling

Try a little snorkeling here. It's fairly calm most of the time and there are several rocky areas where the fish like to hide. We always seem to have fish swimming with us wherever we decide to snorkel.

Beachcombing

We found our first sand dollar at this beach but most of the shells were scattered and broken. But finding an intact sand dollar confirms what we often say - "You never know what you might find."

Green Papaya Medley

an original recipe from Vicky Wells

1 Large Green Papaya (flesh is still white)
Salt
Pepper
Vegetable Oil
1 Medium Onion, chopped
3-4 Garlic Cloves, chopped (or to taste)
½ Sweet Green Pepper, chopped
½ Sweet Red Pepper, chopped
1 Stalk Celery, chopped
½ Cup Sliced Mushrooms
1 16 oz. Can Diced Tomatoes (plain, Italian or Mexican style)
(you can also used fresh tomatoes if you prefer.)
¼ Cup Grated Cheese (choose Cheddar, Romano or Asiago)

We tend to get an overabundance of papaya at our house and found that we like it much better as a vegetable than as a fruit. Here's how we like to prepare it.

Peel, seed and dice papaya. Should be about 4 cups when diced.

Boil diced papaya in salted water for about 20 minutes, drain.

While papaya is boiling, place about 2 Tablespoons of oil in large frying pan. Heat over medium-high heat. Add chopped onion, garlic and celery and brown slightly.

Add drained papaya, red and green pepper and sauté for about five minutes.

Add sliced mushrooms and sauté a couple of minutes longer.

Add diced tomatoes complete with juice from the can.

Cook over medium heat for about five minutes. Salt and pepper to taste.

Sprinkle grated cheese over the top and allow cheese to melt slightly.

Serve immediately.

Current - West Side

N 25° 24.666'~W 76° 47.258'

REVISED: Most of the access to this beach is obstructed by private property. There is an access point where you can park in the shade and walk over a few, even rocks to get to the beach. The shore can be rocky in places but there are some nice sandy beaches - mostly beige sand, a little coarse. Please, always respect other people's private property.

Directions to Current

At 10 miles (16.1 kms) north of **The Cove** turn left at T-junction and right at next T-junction. This puts you on the road to Current. Look for signs to the settlement of Current. If you miss your turns, just ask someone and they'll be sure to point you in the right direction.

Directions to access road - heading north

15.8 miles (25.4 kms) north of **The Cove** turn right. That's just 0.7 miles (1.12 kms) past the **Welcome To Current** sign.

Leave the highway at N 25° 24.495'~W 76° 46.931'

and continue for 0.5 miles (0.8 kms). Then take road to your left for 0.2 miles (0.3 kms).

Access

There is good road almost all the way to the beach. You will encounter a few potholes here and there, however, so stay alert. But with reasonable care any car can make this trip.

Privacy

This beach has many houses on it - don't expect any privacy here. Although, like most beaches in Eleuthera, you will rarely encounter others on the beach. But be sure to be courteous of other people's private property.

Swimming

There can be some pretty strong waves here and the bottom is a little uneven in spots - exercise some caution if you plan to go swimming. On windy days the water can get quite rough. Remember you're on the Atlantic side. Personally, we wouldn't swim here.

Snorkeling

If you do try snorkeling here be sure to try it on a calm day. We wouldn't want you to get pushed up against the rocks. Again, remember you're on the Atlantic side. It can get pretty rough, so exercise caution.

Beachcombing

We didn't find many shells here but a determined beachcomber might find a few good specimens.

Carambola (Star Fruit) Tarts

an original recipe from Vicky Wells

Enough Pastry for 24 tarts or 24 frozen tart shells thawed
1¼ Cups Sugar
2½ Tablespoons Cornstarch
¼ Teaspoon Salt
¼ Cup Water
4½ to 5 Cups Diced Carambola (approximately 7-9 fruits depending on size)
½ Tablespoon Lime Juice

Wash Carambola, remove any brown or damaged parts. Slice crosswise (so you get several star-shaped slices). Remove any seeds. Dice.

Combine sugar, cornstarch and salt in saucepan. Add water and mix well. Add diced fruit and mix well making sure sugar mixture is well distributed through the fruit.

Bring to a boil over medium heat and boil for 2 minutes.

Let cool for 10-15 minutes and add 1/2 tablespoon lime juice. Mix well.

Pour into tart shells.

Bake in a hot oven - 425 deg. F. - for about 15-20 minutes or until pastry is nicely browned.

Our thanks to The Duck Inn for supplying the Carambola fruit from their extensive gardens so that we could develop this recipe.

Current Club Beach

N 25° 24.402'~W 76° 46.843'

REVISED: This beach is pretty easy to find and has a boat launch ramp, as well. The sand is cool, pink and powdery. This is the site of the old Current Club. You can still see some of the old foundations, but that's about all that's left of it. The settlement of Current was, of course, named for the current that flows through the cut between the mainland of Eleuthera and Current Island. It is a popular spot for experienced divers to take a drift dive pushed along by the almost constant current.

Directions to Current

At 10 miles (16.1 kms) north of **The Cove** turn left at T-junction and right at next T-junction. This puts you on the road to Current. If you miss your turns, just stop and ask someone. They'll be happy to point you in the right direction.

Directions to access road - heading north

15.8 miles (25.4 kms) north of **The Cove** turn left. That's just 0.65 miles (1.05 kms) past the **Welcome To Current** sign.

Leave the highway at N 25° 24.499'~W 76° 46.925'

and continue for 0.1 miles (0.2 kms) directly to the beach.

Access

This beach is easily accessible. There is paved road right to the beach and the beach is visible from Queen's Highway. But, if you happen to lose your way, just stop and ask someone and we're sure they'll be happy to point you in the right direction.

Privacy

This beach is right in the settlement of Current. There are many houses overlooking the beach, so don't expect any privacy here. However, you may still have the beach all to yourselves.

Swimming

The water is shallow for a long way out and the bottom is even and sandy. The water is calm most of the time and you'll feel the current that this settlement was named for. If you take water toys or a rubber raft with you, be mindful of the current!

Snorkeling

There should be some good snorkeling around the rocky areas. But, as mentioned above, be mindful of the current. While you're enjoying your snorkeling, you could be moved down the beach a long ways.

Beachcombing

We found a lot of broken shells at this beach but a few good specimens as well. Also, you will often find piles of conch shells in the water left by the fishermen.

Piña Colada Baked Custard

an original recipe from Vicky Wells

2 Ripe Bananas, sliced
6 Large Eggs
¼ Teaspoon Salt
⅓ Cup Packed Brown Sugar
3 Cups Milk
1½ Teaspoons Vanilla Extract
Chopped Fresh Pineapple
Grated Fresh Coconut
Mint Leaves or Wafer-type Cookies for Garnish

Place banana slices in large bowl and mash well using electric mixer on slow speed.

Add eggs and continue to beat on slow speed until eggs and bananas are well incorporated.

Continue beating on slow and gradually add salt and brown sugar. Then, gradually beat in milk and vanilla extract.

Pour into greased, individual custard cups or greased 1-1/2 quart casserole. Place dish(es) in oven-proof pan and fill pan with hot water to within 1 inch of top of custard dish(es).

Bake at 325 deg. F. for about 1 hour, until knife inserted in center comes out clean.

Note: If using one large dish, you may have to increase baking time by 20-30 minutes.

Remove from oven and allow to cool. Refrigerate.

Prior to serving, top with chopped fresh Pineapple and grated fresh coconut. Garnish with wafer-type cookies or mint leaves.

Makes 6-8 Servings

N 25° 24.247'~W 76° 47.102'

REVISED: You need to do a little walking over rocks to get to this beach from the place where you'll park, but it's not difficult. The water is calm and shallow and you can float with the current in a relatively safe place. The white sand bottom can be a bit mushy in places. There's lot's of shade here under the trees.

Head a little further down the road and you'll also find two small, sandy coves.

If you continue along the sandy road you will find the ferry dock and further still an old dock that has some snorkeling possibilities.

Directions to Current

At 10 miles (16.1 kms) north of **The Cove** turn left at T-junction and right at next T-junction. This puts you on the road to Current.

Directions to access road - heading north

16.0 miles (25.7 kms) north of **The Cove** the paved road ends. Continue on the sandy road. This is just 0.85 moles (1.36 kms) past the **Welcome To Current** sign.

Leave the highway at N 25° 24.361'~W 76° 47.041'

and continue on the sandy road for 0.1 miles (0.2 kms). On your left is the remnants of a marina. You can pull in here and park in the shade.

Access

The road to this beach is well used because it leads to the Current dock. It is accessible by a regular sedan but exercise some caution - there are a few rough spots. Take it slow and you'll be fine.

Privacy

There are always boats going by and there are houses that can be seen from these beaches. You may have the beach to yourself but you'll certainly be visible to the boaters.

Swimming

It's pretty calm here but you can definitely feel the Current that comes through Current Cut. It's also a great place to just sit in the water and enjoy the both the current and the view.

Snorkeling

Not much in the way of snorkeling but give it a try if you have the equipment with you. There may be a few interesting spots. Maybe some of the colorful tropical fish will join you.

Beachcombing

We found a few broken shells here, but keep you eyes open, you might find some interesting specimens.

Cistern Cay Beach

N 25° 27.845'~W 76° 39.053'

Although this beach is not very wide (approximately 2500 ft. long x 50 ft. wide), it does have soft, powdery white sand. Walk north and you will discover two smaller beaches. The best way to get to them is to walk in the water. The northern most one is better, so press on. There are a few shady spots along the shore.

Directions to access road - heading south

4.0 miles (6.5 kms) south of **North Eleuthera Texaco**. (See Note (2) below for complete directions.)

Directions to access road - heading north

7.0 miles (11.2 kms) north of **The Cove** turn right onto a dirt road. (see Note (1) below).

Leave the highway at N 25° 27.143'~W 76° 39.773'

and travel 1.2 miles (1.9 kms) along this access road directly to the beach, bypass any side roads. **Note (1):** Coming from the south you'll be making almost a 180 deg turn. **Note (2):** Coming from **North Eleuthera Texaco** take the first left at 1.0 miles (1.7 kms) onto Skyline Dr. and then left again back onto Queen's Hwy. Stay on Queen's Hwy until you reach the access road.

Access

The access road is good with only one particularly rough spot. Keep your eyes open for the rough spot, take it slow and with reasonable care, any car can make it all the way to this beach.

Privacy

This seems to be a fairly secluded beach, however, it is right across from Harbour Island and you're likely to see boaters. Some houses are being built where the access road meets the beach. But the last time we were there construction seemed to be on hold.

Swimming

This is a good place to go swimming. It is almost always calm and it is fairly shallow for a good distance out. However there is some vegetation in the water and the bottom is mushy where there's vegetation.

Snorkeling

There should be some interesting snorkeling around the rocky areas. It is also within view of Cistern Cay, a popular snorkeling spot. As always, it's best to pick a calm day to snorkel.

Beachcombing

We came back from this beach with a couple of nice specimens but you really have to look for them.

Boiling Hole

N25° 26.466' ~ W76° 36.531'

NEW: The Boiling Hole is a bowl cut into the cliff, topped by an impressive natural rock bridge formation. During the changes in tides, this hole does indeed, appear to boil. Located between the Glass Window Bridge and the road to Whale Point it is not hard to find - if you know where to look. It's about 160 ft. in from the highway across smoothed over rock, with little vegetation. You can get down into part of the bowl, but be very, very careful. A rogue wave would be all it would take to wash you out to sea. It is the most impressive, and the most dangerous, at high tide.

Directions to access road - heading south

7.5 miles (12.1 kms) south of **North Eleuthera Texaco**, pull off onto the road to Whale Point, on your left (see the directions to Bottom Harbour Beach opposite).

Directions to access road - heading north

0.4 miles (0.6 kms) north of **The Glass Window Bridge**, pull of onto the road To Whale Point, on your right (see the directions to Bottom Harbour Beach opposite).

Leave the highway at N 25° 26.440'~W 76° 36.526'

After parking at Whale Point Road, walk towards the Glass Window Bridge for approximately 265 ft. to the above GPS reading, then head towards the Atlantic for approximately 165 ft. It's difficult to see until you are almost on top of it, so be careful.

Access

It's just off the Queen's Highway so car access is fine, walking can be tricky on the sharp coral. Please no flip flops here.

Bottom Harbour Beach

N 25° 27.436'~W 76° 37.531'

This is a nice beach for a long stroll. With the Bottom Harbour Beach Club nearby you could sit on their deck, sipping your favorite tropical drink, and enjoying the view. Unfortunately, Bottom Harbour Beach Club is not always open, but the beach is always there. So there's always a reason to visit.

Directions to access road - heading south

7.5 miles (12.1 kms) south of **North Eleuthera Texaco**. (See complete directions below.)

Directions to access road - heading north

3.5 miles (5.7 kms) north of **The Cove** turn right onto the first road past the Glass Window Bridge.

Leave the highway at N 25° 26.462'~W 76° 36.585'

and continue for 1.9 miles (3.0 kms) directly to the beach.

Note: Coming south from **North Eleuthera Texaco** take the first left at 1.0 miles (1.7 kms) onto Skyline Dr. and then left again back onto Queen's Hwy. Stay on Queen's Hwy until you reach the access road.

Access

There are quite a few pot holes on this road, but take it easy and any car can make it. Whale Point is being developed so the road may be much better by the time you read this. But such things move slowly, so be prepared to drive carefully.

Privacy

This beach is right at the Bottom Harbour Beach Club Restaurant and Bar. This is a popular spot so don't expect any privacy on the beach. You may frequently see boaters at this beach as well.

Swimming

The water is shallow and calm - an ideal spot to do some swimming, so don't forget your bathing suit. Parts of the bottom can be a bit mushy, but all-in-all it's a pleasant place to be.

Snorkeling

There should be some good snorkeling here. We've also been told that the snorkeling is good around Cistern Cay. That's the big rock you can see out in the harbour not far from Whale Point.

Beachcombing

We didn't find as many shells here as we did at the old hotel site (see the next page), but look around, you just might find something.

Glass Window Bridge

N25° 26.259' ~ W76° 36.259'

NEW: The natural stone bridge formation spanning the narrowest part of Eleuthera was destroyed by the wind and waves of a hurricane. It has been replaced by a concrete bridge which is itself showing some wear and tear. The single lane bridge still supports traffic, including heavy construction trucks, so you needn't worry about taking a car safely across it. The main attraction here is seeing the deep blue, often rough waters of the Atlantic pour through into the calm, turquoise waters of the sound. The Glass Window was so named because ships being tossed about on the Atlantic could peer through the "window" and see the perfectly calm waters on the other side.

Directions to access road - heading south

7.7 miles (12.3 kms) south of **North Eleuthera Texaco**, pull off onto the small area on your left, just before entering the bridge.

Directions to access road - heading north

3.0 miles (4.8 kms) north of **The Cove**, pull off onto the small area on the north side of the bridge.

Leave the highway at N 25° 26.259'~W 76° 36.259'

The Glass Window Bridge is actually part of the Queen's Highway. You don't need to leave the highway at all to visit this popular and "must see" attraction.

Access

Access to this attraction is not a problem for any car, as it is right on Queen's Highway. There are a few potholes and some areas of broken pavement, so stay alert, but The Glass Window Bridge is easy to get to.

Whale Point Beach

N 25° 28.066'~W 76° 37.548'

Although this beach is designated as being on the Atlantic side it is actually part of a very well protected bay created by Harbour Island and Whale Point. But it can sometimes get pretty rough in the bay when there's bad weather. If you're a boater this bay is ideal and both this beach and the one at Bottom Harbour make excellent picnic spots.

Directions to access road - heading south

7.5 miles (12.1 kms) south of **North Eleuthera Texaco**. Turn left just before the Glass Window Bridge.

Directions to access road - heading north

3.5 miles (5.7 kms) north of **The Cove** turn right onto the first road pasted the Glass Window Bridge.

Leave the highway at N 25° 26.462'~W 76° 36.585'

and go 1.4 miles (2.2 kms) then turn right just before the **Bottom Harbour Beach Club**. Follow the road around the bend until you get to a stone entrance in front of an old hotel. Turn left at the entrance and go just around the corner to a parking area. You should see some overgrown concrete steps that will take you to the beach. Total distance from the Hwy 2.4 miles (3.8 kms).

Access

There are quite a few potholes on this road, but take it easy and any car can make it. Whale Point is being developed so the road may be much better by the time you read this. But these kind of things move slowly, so be prepared to exercise caution.

Privacy

There are a few houses down this road but we've never seen anyone on this beach. As this is in the harbour created by Whale Point, Harbour Island and the rest of Eleuthera you're likely to see some boaters.

Swimming

Although it appears, at first, to be an ideal swimming spot, there's a lot of vegetation on the bottom. The bottom can also be a bit "squishy" in spots. The water can also get rough in bad weather, so always pick a calm day.

Snorkeling

There should be some good snorkeling here. We've also been told that the snorkeling is good around Cistern Cay. That's the big rock you can see out in the harbour not far from Whale Point.

Beachcombing

We've brought back a few shells from this beach. Look around. You're likely to find something nice, but you may really have to search for it.

Queen's Baths

N25° 25.446' ~ W76° 35.854'

NEW: These round depressions are a natural formation that allow the ocean waves to enter, swirl around and exit the "baths". You'll need a good pair of shoes and a little determination to get down to them, but with care you'll make it alright. **Caution**: check the tides before you go. The baths can fill up rapidly and forcefully at high tide particularly if you see any white caps on the ocean. It would only take one strong wave to wash you out to sea, so be careful, we hate losing tourists. ☺

Directions to access road - heading south

0.6 miles (0.9 kms) south of the **Glass Window** bridge, turn left onto a sandy road, tucked between several trees.

Directions to access road - heading north

3.0 miles (4.8 kms) north of **The Cove**, turn right onto a sandy road, tucked between several trees.

Leave the highway at N 25° 25.878'~W 76° 35.870'

and continue for 0.05 miles (0.08 kms) along a sandy road with lots of rocky spots. Once parked, head towards the Atlantic and then to your left, carefully heading down towards the baths.

Access

Be sure to have sturdy shoes to get over the rocks down to the baths. Some of the bare coral can be pretty uneven and sharp, but the rocks become much more smooth, from eons of crashing waves, as you get closer to the baths.

N 25° 25.952'~W 76° 36.021'

This small beach offers a lot - good swimming, snorkeling and shelling. Watch for the large boulders called Cow and Bull on the Atlantic side of the Highway, and Maverick at the spot to park. The Twin Sisters are the two large boulders in the water. This may not be the most spectacular beach on the island but it is one we like to visit regularly.

Directions to access road - heading south

8.4 miles (13.5 kms) south of **North Eleuthera Texaco** (See complete directions below.)

Directions to access road - heading north

2.7 miles (4.3 kms) north of **The Cove** watch for a short access road on your left near a large boulder (Maverick).

Leave the highway at N 25° 25.980'~W 76° 35.984'

and the parking spot you are looking for is just off the highway on the Caribbean side just north of a telephone pole.

Note: Coming south from **North Eleuthera Texaco** take the first left at 1.0 miles (1.7 kms) onto Skyline Dr. and then left again back onto Queen's Hwy. Stay on Queen's Hwy until you reach the access road.

Access

This beach is easily accessible right off Queen's Highway and has a convenient place to park with a wide path down to the beach. Depending on how much vegetation growth there is when you visit, the parking spot might be hard to see, so keep your eyes pealed.

Privacy

From time to time we have seen other people at the beach. Other times we have had it all to ourselves. However, there are almost always fresh footprints in the sand. So you can't expect to always have this beach to yourselves.

Swimming

This is a great place to go swimming. The water is calm, clear and relatively shallow and the bottom is soft white sand once you get past a few rocks at the shoreline. The water can kick up a bit on windy days, but it is still pleasant.

Snorkeling

There is some terrific snorkeling around the two big boulders (the Twin Sisters) out in the water, as well as around groups of rocks just to the north and south of the beach. We've often had some of the colorful fish swim along with us.

Beachcombing

This is one of the best shelling beaches we have found. We almost always bring some shells back from here to add to our shell garden.

Gaulding Cay Beach

N 25° 25.412'~W 76° 35.611'

This popular Caribbean side beach is a great place to pack a picnic lunch and go for a day of swimming, snorkeling and relaxing. There is a place to park and shade is available if you want it. The sand is soft, smooth and powdery. The Cove, a resort not far from here, frequently offers its guests day trips to this beach. It's generally calm and fairly shallow for a good distance out.

Directions to access road - heading south

9.0 miles (14.6 kms) south of **North Eleuthera Texaco**. (See complete directions below.)

Directions to access road - heading north

2.0 miles (3.2 kms) north of **The Cove**. Turn left at the sandy access road.

Leave the highway at N 25° 25.546'~W 76° 35.502'

and go 0.2 miles (0.3 kms), keeping left at the "Y" in the road. There is also a "private road" sign, but this is the right road. Keep going past the house to the beach. Note: Coming south from **North Eleuthera Texaco** take the first left at 1.0 miles (1.7 kms) onto Skyline Dr. and then left again back onto Queen's Hwy. Stay on Queen's Hwy until you reach the access road on your right.

Access

With reasonable care this beach can be accessed by any car along a sandy road. There are several dips and bumps along the way. Just take it slow and easy and you shouldn't have any trouble.

Privacy

This is a popular beach and there are several houses right on the beach. You'll almost always find someone at this beach, so don't expect any privacy when you visit. Also, remember to respect the private property of the homeowners here.

Swimming

This beach is a good choice if you want to do some swimming. The water is shallow and calm. The bottom is sandy and even. Always keep an eye to the weather. Even the Caribbean side can get rough from time to time.

Snorkeling

You'll find good snorkeling around the rocky areas and around the large rock out in the water. We were once joined by a playful Ray. Enjoy the sea life you encounter but remember they are wild creatures and be sure to give them their "space".

Beachcombing

We have found some nice shells here but you really have to keep your eyes open. So take the time to look around and you might go home with something really nice.

Hideaway Beach

N25° 25.332' ~ W76° 35.581'

NEW: Tucked between a subdivision and a private residence, the road to this beach can be easy to miss. There is currently construction going on here for a new resort complex and restaurant called The Beach. We have spoken to the owner and you are welcome to use the road. Once the restaurant is finished this will be a terrific place to spend the day.

The beach is in a small, curving bay and is almost always calm as it is on the Caribbean side. The sand is soft and the water shallow for a long way out.

Directions to access road - heading south

1.3 miles (2.1 kms) south of the Glass Window Bridge, turn right onto a sandy road. If you pass a large concrete building on your right, you've missed the road by just a bit.

Directions to access road - heading north

1.75 miles (2.8 kms north of The Cove, turn left onto a sandy road. Look for a large concrete building just before your left turn.

Leave the highway at N 25° 25.412'~W 76° 35.428'

and proceed for 0.2 miles (0.3 kms) and then turn left. The beach will be right in front of you.

Access

The road to this beach is sandy and fairly flat. Just watch out for the odd bump or dip along the way. Any car could negotiate this road. - just proceed slowly and cautiously and you shouldn't have any trouble. I'm sure the road will get upgraded as part of the new construction.

Privacy

Like many beaches on Eleuthera, you can't see this one from the road. It's no wonder it's called Hideaway Beach. However, with residences and a restaurant being built, don't expect any privacy.

Swimming

Being a Caribbean side beach, the water is normally calm and shallow. Swimming here would be pleasant. Always look to the weather, though. Even the Caribbean side can get rough from time to time.

Snorkeling

We have yet to snorkel at this beach, but hope to soon. If you've got your snorkel gear with you, there's no reason you shouldn't give it a try and see what there might be. We've often run into starfish on the Caribbean side.

Beachcombing

We didn't find much in the way of shells or any other beachcombing items at this beach. Still, it's a nice place for quick visit if you're already in the area.

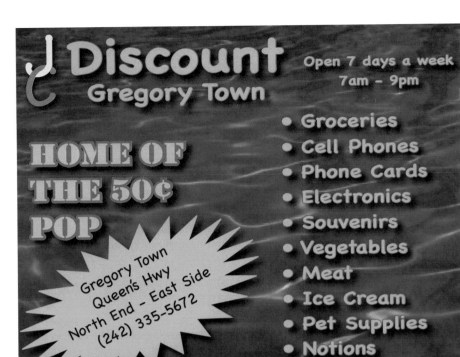

BANYAN TREE

N25° 25.217' ~ W76° 35.467'

Unfortunately, access to this beach, from the road anyway, is restricted. If you want to visit this beach you'll have to get to it by boat. This is one of the best beaches on Eleuthera. It has soft, powdery, white sand and the water is calm and shallow for a long way out. We have been told that this is also referred to locally as Nude Beach. We believe it got this designation because it is very secluded and, before access was restricted, it was still very difficult to get to. As always, we encourage you to respect other people's property and not trespass on restricted land.

Directions Going North

1.6 miles (2.6 kms) north of **The Cove**, you can pull off the highway to your left at the gates and perhaps catch a glimpse of this beach in the distance.

Directions Going South

1.5 miles (2.4 kms) south of **The Glass Window Bridge**, you can pull off the highway to your right at the gates and perhaps catch a glimpse of this beach in the distance.

Leave the highway at N 25° 25.280'~W 76° 35.390'

As mentioned above, the access road to this beach is gated. If you'd like to visit this beach, you'll need to go by boat.

Access

As mentioned above, you can only access this beach by boat. The property has been fenced and gated. As, always, we encourage you to respect private property.

Privacy

If you do come to this beach by boat, you will likely find that you have it all to yourselves. That is, however, until building begins here. We understand that a private residence will be built on this beach.

Swimming

Being a Caribbean side beach with calm, shallow water, this is a great place to go swimming. You may, however, find that you need to be a long way from the shoreline for it to get deep enough for swimming.

Snorkeling

You'd think that this would be a good place for snorkeling because the water is calm and shallow, but we didn't notice much here. But you never know from day to day what you might see.

Beachcombing

We're always on the lookout for shells and other items that might wash ashore. Unfortunately we didn't find much at this beach but such things can change on an almost daily basis.

The Bahamas' Largest Property Showcase

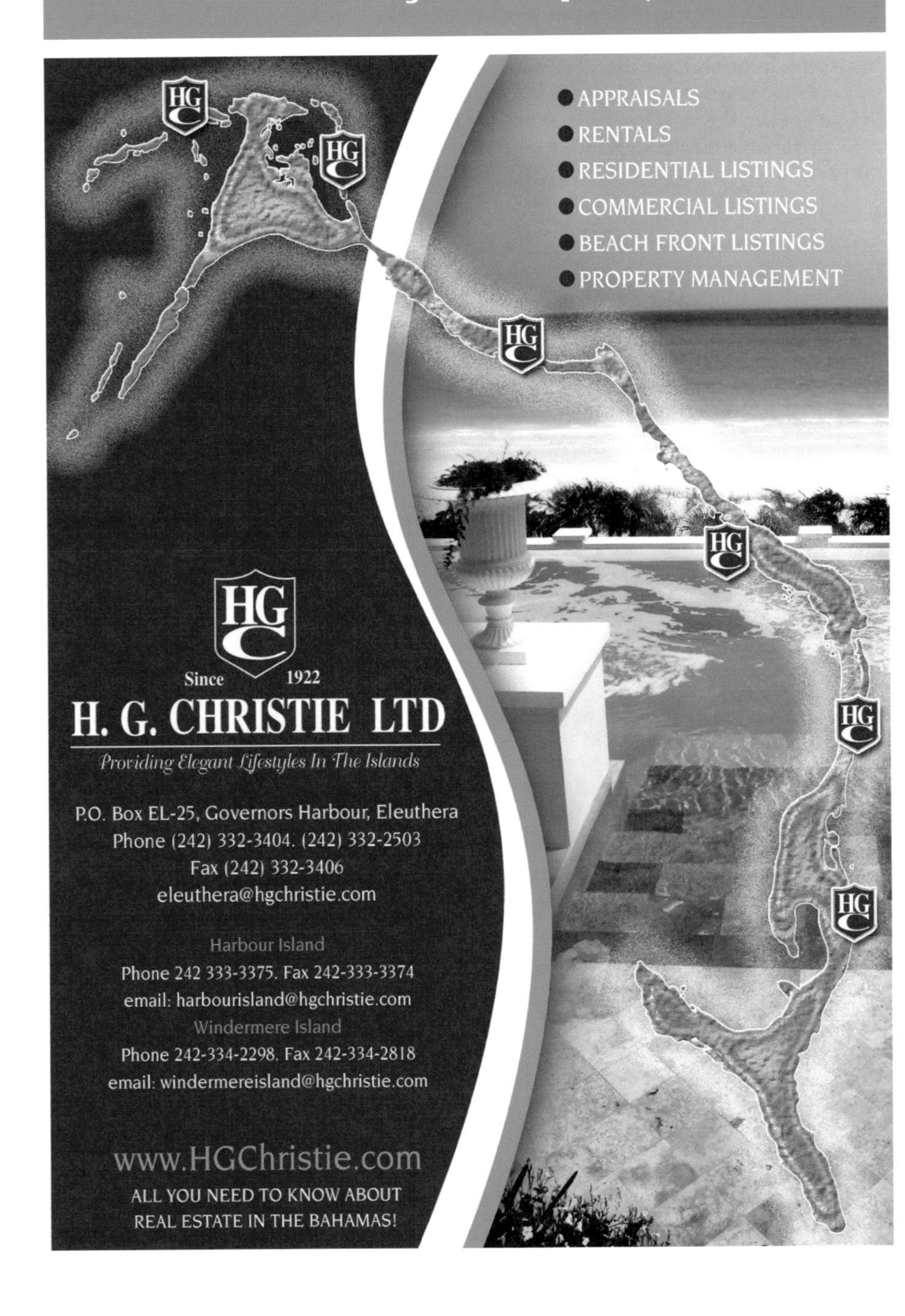

N 25° 25.214'~W 76° 34.064'

This long, wide beach takes some effort to get to but you'll be rewarded by normally having the entire beach all to yourself. If we were going to give any beach a five for privacy, this would be it. You can see the beach from the cliffs where you'll park. Be sure to bring your camera to get some great pictures of breaking Atlantic waves and panoramic beach shots.

Directions to access road - heading south

2.2 miles (3.5 kms) south of **The Glass Window Bridge**, turn left on to the gravel road running between the salt ponds.

Directions to access road - heading north

0.7 miles (1.1 kms) north of **The Cove**, turn right on the gravel road running between the salt ponds.

Leave the highway at N 25° 24.596'~W 76° 34.810'

and proceed for 1.0 miles (1.7 kms). Walk to the edge of the cliff (not too close now) and you'll see the beach. It takes just a few minutes to walk along the rocks and get to this secluded beach.

Access

An SUV is recommended for this road. There is a particularly rough hill about a third of the way in. After parking you'll have to walk over some sharp rocks to get to the beach, so make sure you're wearing some sturdy shoes.

Privacy

If any beach deserves a five privacy rating this is it. It's a fairly large beach and we've never seen anyone else here. It's rare to even find footprints. But we can't guarantee you will have it all to yourselves because after all we found it and so can you.

Swimming

There is a very strong undertow and the bottom drops away quickly. We would not recommend swimming here but it's a great sunbathing beach. So, bring a beach blanket and soak up some rays.

Snorkeling

As with the swimming, we would not recommend snorkeling here. The wave action can be very strong even on calm days. So don't risk ruining your day by taking chances to snorkel here.

Beachcombing

We found some terrific shells here. You could combine your sunbathing with shell hunting. You'll also find all matter of flotsam and jetsam washed up here - maybe even a message in a bottle.

Island Made

Gregory Town

- Eleuthera T-Shirts
- Hand Painted T-Shirts
- Driftwood Painting
- Native Arts & Crafts
- Jewelry

- Bahamian Music
- Androsia Clothing
- Shells & Sea Glass

Shop The Island

- Hand Crafted Dolls
- Native Straw Work
- Jams & Jellies
- Post Cards
- Hot Sauce
- Maps

9am til 5pm
Mon to Sat
(242) 335-5369

Island Made

North Eleuthera Airport

Holiday Beach

N 25° 24.501'~W 76° 33.285'

REVISED: This is a small but pleasant beach. It is rocky in a few spots and the sand can be loose and gravelly. Unfortunately, this is not a particularly good walking beach. However, the rocky outcropping to the north of the beach provides an interesting photo opportunity as waves crash over it. So, be sure to bring your camera along. Depending on the weather conditions the waves can be quite spectacular. Getting to this beach will take you by several houses and a small subdivision.

Directions to access road - heading south

1.0 miles (1.5 kms) south of **The Cove** turn left onto a wide, sandy road.

Directions to access road - heading north

0.4 miles (0.7 kms) north of **Pam's Island Made Gift Shop** turn right onto a wide, sandy road.

Leave the highway at N 25° 23.851'~W 76° 33.542'

and continue for 1.0 miles (1.5 kms) to the beach. Follow the main track. It takes a 90 degree turn to the left just over the hill and further on it takes a 90 degree turn to the right and then continues straight to the beach.

Access

In the last edition we reported that this road was in very bad repair. It seems to have been repaired now, but we still recommend an SUV or something with good ground clearance. There are houses along this road, so we do expect it to be repaired, but aren't sure when.

Privacy

Given that this is currently a difficult beach to get to we have rated it high for privacy. However, there are two houses overlooking the beach and we did find footprints, so don't be surprised is you encounter others here.

Swimming

Being an Atlantic side beach there can be strong waves, sharp drop-offs and undertow. We wouldn't recommend swimming. If you choose to go swimming here please exercise extreme caution.

Snorkeling

Because of the waves, we don't recommend snorkeling at this beach. Hey, there are lots of other places to snorkel, so don't get discouraged. It's not worth ruining your day to get tossed against some rocks by a rogue wave.

Beachcombing

There are lots of shells here but most of them are broken or very small. However, there are lots of other beachcombing items washed up on this beach.

Surfers Beach

N 25° 22.893'~W 76° 31.579'

If this is not the most famous beach on Eleuthera, it is most likely the second most famous. However, that doesn't mean it's the easiest beach to find. The surf is best when the wind is blowing from the Caribbean side. Be sure to bring your camera as the surf breaking along the miles of beach makes for spectacular photographs. Look for a couple of makeshift shaded seats with magnificent views and several well worn trails down the dunes to the beach.

Directions to access road - heading south

2.0 miles (3.3 kms) south of **Pam's Island Made Gift Shop** turn left at the gravel road.

Directions to access road - heading north

5.9 miles (9.5 kms) north of the **Rainbow Inn** turn right at the gravel road.

Leave the highway at N 25° 22.424'~W 76° 31.858'

and go 0.7 miles (1.1 kms) to the beach. There is a concrete house with a red roof on the southeast corner of the Queen's Hwy. On the way to the beach you'll pass a new resort called **Surfers Beach Manor**. At the bottom of the hill is a T-junction. Turn left. The next road on your right (a sandy road) is the access road to the beach.

Access

At the very least, make sure your car has good clearance. Although a 4WD vehicle is not necessary, adequate clearance and caution is. Or you can park at **Surfers Beach Manor** and walk.

Privacy

This is a very popular beach - particularly with surfers. Don't expect much privacy here. There will be times when you're the only people on the beach, but it is likely that others will show up while you're there.

Swimming

The large waves are what makes this beach so popular with surfers. Unless you are a strong swimmer we suggest you confine your swimming to the small cove at the north end of the beach (see Kiddie Pool).

Snorkeling

There is a small cove at the north end of the beach that is good for snorkeling on very calm days. Other than that, this beach is not recommended for snorkeling. As always, keep on eye to the weather.

Beachcombing

This beach boasts lots of shells but most are broken. However, you're likely to find all manner of items washed up on this shore. We have often taken some special finds home with us from shells, to fishing nets and even some lumber.

KIDDIE POOL

N 25° 23.033'~W 76° 31.666'

NEW: The Kiddie Pool is actually a part of Surfers Beach, but we give this section a special mention for those of us who are not surfers or strong swimmers, but would still like to get into the water at this popular beach. Because this section, at the North end of the beach, is well protected by a large coral rock head, it is mostly calm. There are still some pretty impressive waves that crash on the ocean side of the rock but they are dampened to ripples in the pool and so makes this a good place for kids to play.

Directions to access road - heading south

2.0 miles (3.3 kms) south of **Pam's Island Made Gift Shop** turn left at the gravel road.

Directions to access road - heading north

5.9 miles (9.5 kms) north of the **Rainbow Inn** turn right at the gravel road.

Leave the highway at N 25° 22.424'~W 76° 31.858'

and go 0.7 miles (1.1 kms) to the beach. There is a concrete house with a red roof on the southeast corner of the Queen's Hwy. On the way to the beach you'll pass a new resort called **Surfers Beach Manor**. At the bottom of the hill is a T-junction. Turn left. The next road on your right (a sandy road) is the access road to the beach.

Access

At the very least, make sure your car has good clearance. Although a 4WD vehicle is not necessary, adequate clearance and caution is. Or you can park at **Surfers Beach Manor** and walk.

Privacy

This is a very popular beach – particularly with surfers. Don't expect much privacy here. There will be times when you're the only people on the beach, but it is likely that others will show up while you're there. We've only been there a couple of times when there's been no one but us.

Swimming

Although this is probably not a very good place for swimming because you simply don't have much room to do that, it's a great place to just "get wet" and enjoy the water and the gentle waves.

Snorkeling

This is not a place where we would recommend snorkeling. Although most of the waves are dampened by the coral rocks, some energetic waves still get through. So if you try snorkeling here, keep well inside the rock head.

Beachcombing

As with Surfers Beach, you'll find lots of broken shells here along with the odd gem. But, mostly you'll find other things washed ashore such as plastic contains, intact glass bottles, bits of wood to name a few. Be sure to watch where you walk in bare feet.

Hatchet Bay Caves

N25° 21.998' ~ W76° 31.212'

NEW: At press time the Hatchet Bay Caves were closed for restoration. The Caves consist of many chambers and continue right out to a cliff face overlooking the Caribbean side of the island. If you plan to visit the Caves, check and see if they are open again. You can always check in Alice Town/Hatchet Bay to see if there are any guides available to give you a tour of the Caves, if they have been re-opened.

Directions to access road - heading south

3.0 miles (4.8 kms) south of **Pam's Island Made Gift Shop** turn right onto a sandy track.

Directions to access road - heading north

5.0 miles (8.0 kms) north of **Rainbow Inn** turn left onto a sandy track..

Leave the highway at N 25° 22.076'~W 76° 31.118'

and proceed for 740 feet (225 meters) to the mouth of the Caves.

Access

Access is right off the Queen's Highway, so any car can make it. There may be a few bumps and dips on the sandy road after you leave the highway. Just go slow and exercise some caution and you'll be fine. There's a large, flat area near the mouth of the Caves where you can park your car.

N 25° 20.916'~W 76° 28.718'

Alice Town Beach is a bit gravelly but nestled in a large, curving bay. If you're in the settlement of Alice Town/Hatchet Bay, be sure to check this out for swimming, snorkeling and shelling. Getting to this beach gives you a quick tour of Alice Town. There's a Post Office, Clinic and Police Office in Alice Town. There's also some grocery stores and several other stores, so take the time to explore this settlement while you're also looking for the beach.

Directions to access road - heading south

5.3 miles (8.6 kms) south of **Pam's Island Made Gift Shop** turn right into Alice Town/Hatchet Bay.

Directions to access road - heading north

2.6 miles (4.2 kms) north of the **Rainbow Inn** take the left turn into Alice Town/ Hatchet Bay.

Leave the highway at N 25° 21.054'~W 76° 29.083'

and take the first road on your left after leaving Queen's Highway. Follow this road all the way around to a T-junction ending at Seven Gables cottage and turn left to the beach.

Access

This is an easy-to-access beach with paved road all the way. Remember as you make all the turns that in the Bahamas, we drive on the left side of the road. It's easy to forget after making a turn.

Privacy

This beach is right in the settlement of Alice Town. Even though we didn't run into anyone while we were visiting this beach, don't expect any privacy here. There are also several houses very close to this beach.

Swimming

The bottom is sandy and the water is calm, clear and shallow, most of the time, making this a good spot for a swim. As always, keep your eye on the weather because even the Caribbean side can get rough from time to time.

Snorkeling

Given the number of shells we found on this beach, the snorkeling should be pretty good. If you've brought your snorkel gear with you, go ahead and give it a try. You might be pleasantly surprised.

Beachcombing

There are lots of shells here but most of them are broken. Keep your eyes open, you may find some good specimens.

Sweeting's Pond

N 25° 21.520'~W 76° 30.272'

REVISED: This is a landlocked, saltwater pond, not a beach, but it is an interesting place to visit. Local legend has it that a giant octopus inhabits this Sweeting's Pond. Others believe it may be a large moray eel. Nonetheless, it is a very unusual area with tulip shells, brittle stars and the occasional small octopus. Jacques Cousteau was interested in this pond and made a few dives here many years ago. You can also Google Sweeting's Pond for some interesting scientific studies and reports on the creatures that inhabit the pond.

Directions to access road - heading south

4.2 miles (6.7 kms) south of **Pam's Island Made Gift Shop** turn right onto a dirt track.

Directions to access road - heading north

3.8 miles (6.1 kms) north of **Rainbow Inn** turn left onto a dirt track.

Leave the highway at N 25° 21.640'~W 76° 30.061'

and proceed for 0.25 miles (0.4 kms) to the pond. **Note:** there are two silos at this road and just across the highway is a gravel pit carved out of the limestone cliff. Watch out for the wrecked car that sticks out onto the path a little way.

Access

This dirt track can be a little rough in a few spots but nothing that a regular car can't handle with reasonable care. Be mindful that you are traveling past someone's farming area. Please be sure not disturb any of the crops growing here.

Privacy

We have never seen anyone else here but there is some farming going on in this area. Please be respectful of others property and their crops. You're here to visit Sweeting's Pond, not someone's farm.

Swimming

It's a nice, clear, saltwater pond, just watch out for the sea urchins. We saw quite a few near the shoreline. Be careful. If you're not comfortable getting in the water here, then you probably shouldn't.

Snorkeling

We understand it is a very interesting place to snorkel, but suggest that you be experienced and a strong swimmer. It gets very deep in the centre so bring your diving gear and pretend you're Jacques Cousteau. See if you can find the giant octopus.

Beachcombing

As this is not a beach, there is nowhere for shells to wash up so don't expect to do any shelling here. However, there are shellfish in this salt water pond.

Note: Thanks to Wayne Rossman for supplying some of the information on this page.

Hatchet Bay Beach

N25° 21.548' ~ W76° 28.207'

NEW: We briefly mentioned this beach in our previous edition. We simply said you'd see another larger beach when you parked to go to Beach for Two. We decided that this large Atlantic side beach deserved it's own mention. This is a long, wide and frequently deserted beach. It seems to stretch on well to the North so you may want to explore the extent of this welcoming stretch of sand and sea. The sand is white and soft underfoot. The sand along the shoreline is fairly compacted, so stick close the water if you plan a long walk.

Directions to access road - heading south

6.3 miles (10.2 kms) south of **Pam's Island Made Gift Shop** turn left onto a dirt track.

Directions to access road - heading north

1.6 miles (2.6 kms) north of **Rainbow Inn** turn right onto a dirt track.

Leave the highway at N 25° 21.305'~W 76° 28.194'

and plow through .025 miles (0.4 kms) of tall grass heading toward the Atlantic side of the island. In the winter it is not too bad but it gets pretty overgrown during the summer.

Access

Access is along a well overgrown road used mostly by farmers, but the road itself is fairly flat and even. Slow down when you're getting close, this road is very easy to miss. Slow down again where the road bends slightly to the left - there's a bit of a drop.

Privacy

It's rare to find anyone else at this beach and if you make the effort to climb over the rocks towards the south you'll find a secluded cove, with a lovely beach and a small cave which we have dubbed "Beach for Two". However, there's always been footprints in the sand whenever we've been there.

Swimming

It gets pretty deep pretty quickly here and there are good waves even on calm days. But just bobbing around in the waves can be a lot of fun. Be sure to be careful, we've had a wave or two knock us down.

Snorkeling

There may be some snorkeling around the rocky areas but we'd suggest you try that only on very, very calm days. We've been told that there is some staghorn coral straight out from the Beach for Two area.

Beachcombing

You're likely to find lots of different items on this beach from boat fenders, to sea glass, to nets and more. But, not a lot of intact shells.

BEACH FOR TWO

N 25° 21.556'~W 76° 28.204'

There are actually several beaches along this stretch of coastline. The access road takes you to a nice, fairly large beach (see previous beach description). The surprise is a couple of hundred feet to your right. Bring your good walking shoes because you'll need to climb over some sharp coral rocks to get to "Beach for Two". That's our name for it and it seems to fit. Don't give up if you can't see the beach right away. After all you'll need to be watching your step most of the way. We actually hesitated putting this one in the book, but didn't feel right keeping it all to ourselves.

Directions to access road - heading south

6.3 miles (10.2 kms) south of **Pam's Island Made Gift Shop** turn left onto a dirt track.

Directions to access road - heading north

1.6 miles (2.6 kms) north of **Rainbow Inn** turn right onto a dirt track.

Leave the highway at N 25° 21.305'~W 76° 28.194'

and plow through 0.25 miles (0.4 kms) of tall grass towards the Atlantic side. In the winter it is not too bad but it gets pretty overgrown during the summer.

Access

Access is along a well overgrown road used mostly by farmers, but the road itself is fairly flat and even. Slow down when you're getting close, this road is very easy to miss. Slow down again where the road bends slightly to the left - there's a bit of a drop that can be hard on your car if you don't take it slowly.

Privacy

It's rare to find anyone else at this beach and if you make the effort to climb over the rocks towards the south you'll find a secluded cove, with a lovely beach and a small cave which we have dubbed "Beach for Two".

Swimming

It gets pretty deep pretty quickly here and there are good waves even on calm days. We couldn't get into swim when we were there once. A storm swept a huge amount of seaweed onto the beach. But it was all gone by our next visit.

Snorkeling

There may be some snorkeling around the rocky areas but we'd suggest you try that only on very, very calm days. We've been told that there is some staghorn coral straight out.

Beachcombing

Although we didn't find a lot of shells in this area, there is still a lot of beach combing possible here. We did score a really nice boat fender on one of our visits.

Twin Beach

N 25° 20.536'~W 76° 26.525'

This unique, absolutely must-see beach is in the popular and well-kept Rainbow Bay subdivision. Don't hesitate to put this on your list of beaches to visit. Most of the roads are paved, so this beach is pretty easy to get to. An access path has been cut right through the cliff face and you will need to climb down a couple of uneven stairs cut into the rock. The cliff overhangs the beach, so there is shade on hot, sunny days. Go around the rocks at the far end of this tiny beach and you'll discover why it's called Twin Beach.

Directions to access road - heading south

0.7 miles (1.1 kms) south of **Rainbow Inn** turn left onto Cross Island Drive.

Directions to access road - heading north

4.7 miles (7.5 kms) north of **James Cistern Pier** turn right onto Cross Island Drive.

Leave the highway at N 25° 20.231'~W 76° 26.350'

and continue on Cross Island Drive for 0.2 miles (0.3 kms) to Ocean Drive. Turn left on Ocean Drive and go 0.4 miles (0.6 kms) to Twin Beach Drive. You'll find a parking area here. The path to the beach is easily missed so don't give up if you don't find it right away. Look for a track in the grass at the south end of the parking area.

Access

There is paved road right to the access path so you have no excuse for not checking this out. So, naturally, any car can get you to this beach. Just watch out for the odd pothole or water on the road.

Privacy

We have encountered other people at this beach from time to time, but have also frequently had to all to ourselves. However, there are always footprints in the sand. It's a popular spot in a popular development.

Swimming

The waves can get quite large. This is more of a bobbing beach than swimming one. We have been told it is a good beach for body surfing. You'll find that the sand will come and go from this beach.

Snorkeling

As the waves are pretty intense most of the time, we would not recommend snorkeling here. According to a friend who has tried snorkeling here, there isn't much to see even if you did try.

Beachcombing

There were a few shells but they were scattered and broken. Don't plan on finding a prize specimen here. Just go to enjoy the uniqueness of the location.

EleutheraLiving
Your island information source
Your Tourism Guide & Local Yellow Pages
Restaurants • Fishing Charters • Art Work & Crafts • Marinas
Vacation Rentals • Construction Resources • Car Rentals • Real Estate
Island Guide • News & Sip Sip • More...
www.eleutheraliving.com

Private Doctors

Name	*Settlement*	*Phone No.*	*Notes*
Dr. Steve Bailey	Spanish Wells (Russell Island)	333-4868 333-4869 (office)	
Dr. Cliff Bacchus	Governor's Harbour	332-2902	
Eleuthera's Pro-Active Health Care Clinic	Upper Bogue	335-1841 335-1842 (Fax)	Specialists come in from Nassau on a regular basis - check with office
Eleuthera Dental Center Dr. Hadassah Knowles DDS	Palmetto Point & Lower Bogue	242-332-1477 242-332-1478 (Fax)	Full dental service
Dr. Peter Bizzell Nassau Office 242-325-1354	Visits regularly: Spanish Wells Palmetto Point Wemyss Bight	Ros Seyfert 242-332-2877 Ruth Whylly 242-334-6350	Veterinary Medicine

Smuggler's Beach

N 25° 20.395'~W 76° 26.130'

This white sand beach is 700 ft. long x 100 ft. deep, but you won't be able to see it from the road. As a matter of fact, you won't be able to see it until you're almost on top of it. There is a well used path with stairs down from the park above. The path and stairs are directly opposite the park entrance. Easy to find once you know where to look but equally easy to miss by a first time visitor. Aren't you glad you have this guide? The stairs can be a bit challenging, so take your time and be careful. After all, you're in paradise now - there's no need to hurry at all. Just enjoy the sun, sand, salt air and warm water.

Directions to access road - heading south

0.7 miles (1.1 kms) south of **Rainbow Inn** turn left onto Cross Island Drive.

Directions to access road - heading north

4.7 miles (7.5 kms) north of **James Cistern Pier** turn right onto Cross Island Drive.

Leave the highway at N 25° 20.231'~W 76° 26.350'

and continue on Cross Island Drive for 0.2 miles (0.3 kms) to Ocean Drive. Turn right on Ocean Drive and go 0.1 miles (0.2 kms) to Smuggler's Beach Park Site. Walk towards the ocean and you'll find a stairway down to the beach.

Access

Any car can make it to access point for this beach. There is paved road all the way to the park site. Then you just need to follow the directions above to find the path down to the beach.

Privacy

We have frequently encountered other people at this beach. Don't expect much privacy. Once you have found it the first time, it is easy to come to again and again - and many people do.

Swimming

As with most beaches on the Atlantic side you need to exercise caution. The waves can be quite strong as can the undertow and the bottom can drop away quickly. Good place to get wet but you won't do much swimming.

Snorkeling

We would not recommend snorkeling at this beach. The waves can be pretty aggressive here, even on calm days. But don't despair, there are lots of other places to go snorkel-ing.

Beachcombing

There are a fair number of shells at this beach. Look around for the best specimens. You will frequently find other beachcombing items here from time to time.

Windy Atlantic

N 25° 20.251'~W 76° 25.460'

REVISED: This popular beach in the Rainbow Bay subdivision is a nice place to stop for a while. You might want to take a walk along the road running along the shoreline to the south. A good portion of it got washed out during Hurricane Andrew and it is an interesting stroll. The last time we were there a lot of the road had been repaired, but you can still get an idea of the power of a hurricane. Also, check out the huge trench dug alongside the road to try to control the waves and water. Come here on windy days and get some spectacular photographs of waves crashing against the rocks as well as some panoramic views of the beach and spectacular ocean waves with whitecaps. You might just get a glimpse of some of the resident "curly tails" lizards, too. Keep your eyes open - they move really fast.

Directions to access road - heading south

1.6 miles (2.6 kms) south of **Rainbow Inn** turn left onto Hidden Beach Road.

Directions to access road - heading north

3.8 miles (6.1 kms) north of **James Cistern Pier** turn right onto Hidden Beach Road.

Leave the highway at N 25° 20.118'~W 76° 25.504'

and proceed for 0.1 miles (0.2 Kms) on Hidden Beach Road directly to the beach.

Access

This beach is easily accessible by any car. There is paved road right to the beach. Many of the roads in the Rainbow Bay subdivision are paved making it easy to get around and explore.

Privacy

Don't count on any privacy. This is a popular spot and there are often other people enjoying a stroll on the beach, swimming, snapping photographs or just enjoying the view. When the wind kicks up you can enjoy the salt spray and wonderful ocean smell.

Swimming

The waterline can be a bit rocky in spots, but the sand is beige and cool. The waves can really kick up here so be careful. It's a great "bobbing and paddling" beach but we're not sure you'd want to do a lot of swimming here.

Snorkeling

Just to the south of this beach is a little rocky cove. You might want to try snorkeling there, on a calm day. We saw our first sea turtle in the wild at this little cove. Always respect the wildlife and be sure to give them their "space".

Beachcombing

There isn't a whole lot in the way of shelling here. But look around - you just never know.

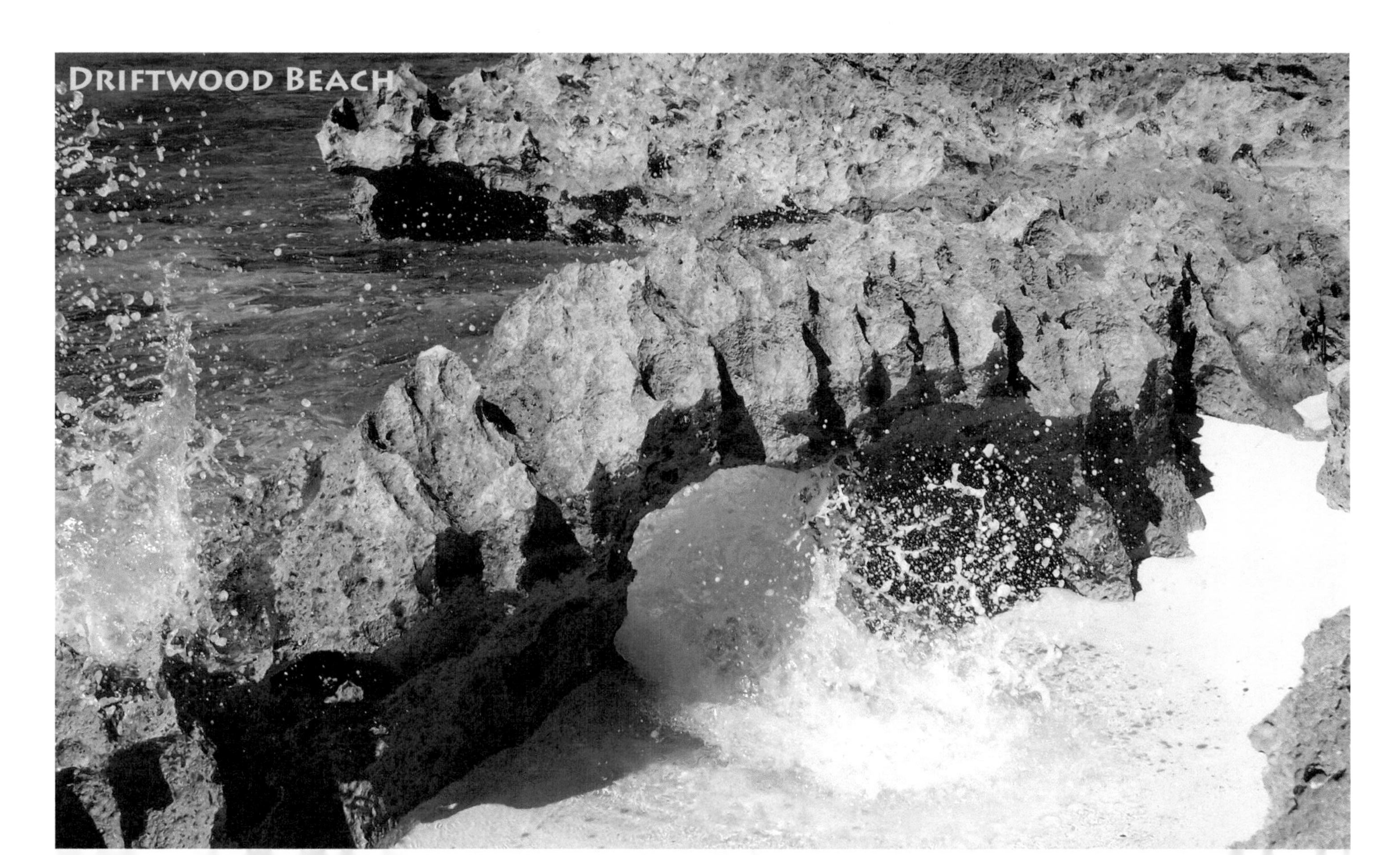
DRIFTWOOD BEACH

Driftwood Beach

N 25° 20.172'~W 76° 25.119'

REVISED: - This postage stamp-sized beach has slightly coarse, loosely packed sand. This beach is also called Come 'N Go Beach (apparently there used to be a sign to that effect), but we dubbed it Driftwood Beach because of the amount of wood that has washed up on shore. On rough days the waves can be quite spectacular. If you walk north along Ocean Drive, you'll see where Hurricane Andrew took out a big chunk of the road. It's pretty impressive. Walk a little bit South over the rock (be sure to have good shoes, the rocks are sharp) and check out the "portal" formation in the water. It's fascinating to watch the waves pour through the portal. You can see a picture of the portal on the opposite page and on our website www.elusivebeaches.com.

Directions to access road - heading south

1.9 miles (3.1 kms) south of **Rainbow Inn** turn left onto Sea to Sea Drive.

Directions to access road - heading north

3.3 miles (5.3 kms) north of **James Cistern Pier** turn right onto Sea to Sea Drive.

Leave the highway at N 25° 20.177'~W 76° 25.185'

and proceed 0.2 miles (0.35 kms), turning left on Ocean Drive and continuing on to the parking area.

Access

This beach is easily accessible by any car. There is paved road all the way. Many of the roads in the Rainbow Bay subdivision are paved. So, just follow the directions, it's easy to find.

Privacy

Although we've never seen anyone else on this beach we have seen lots of footprints. We suspect that many people would drop by to see what the ocean waves have dragged up onto the beach.

Swimming

Given the size of this beach and the fact that it's on the Atlantic side, we wouldn't recommend swimming here. There are some sharp drop-offs and rocky areas, so be careful if you decide to go in the water.

Snorkeling

It would be tough to snorkel here without getting thrown against the rocks and some of the rocks are pretty sharp. We wouldn't recommend snorkeling here. But don't despair. There are lots of other places to snorkel.

Beachcombing

There are lots of shells on this beach but you'll have to search for intact specimens. There's also all kinds of other items washed up on this beach, some of which can be quite interesting and we're sure they'd have stories to tell if they could talk.

The Cliffs

N25° 20.198' ~ W76° 24.529'

NEW: An impressive place to view the Atlantic Ocean, the Cliffs rise dramatically from the sea. A wide path has been cut through the limestone here, making it easy to get to the ocean. If you plan to climb to the top of the Cliffs, be sure to have sturdy shoes. Some of the coral rocks are very sharp and there are lots of holes where you could easily twist your ankle.

You get an amazing view of both the Atlantic and the island from the top of the Cliffs but it can be very windy and there aren't any guard rails - so be careful.

Directions to access road - heading south

2.55 miles (4.1 kms) south of **The Rainbow Inn**, turn left onto a sandy road.

Directions to access road - heading north

2.85 miles (4.6 kms) north of **James Cistern Pier**, turn right onto a sandy road.

Leave the highway at N 25° 19.960'~W 76° 24.557'

and proceed for 0.3 miles (0.5 kms) to the parking area in front of the cut between the cliffs. There is normally a sign pointing to the access road on the West side of Queen's Highway. However, at press time, the sign was down.

Access

The road into the Cliffs is sandy and fairly level. There's also a large, circular, sandy area where you can park your car. Any car can make it to this attraction.

N 25° 20.052'~W 76° 25.891'

REVISED: This is probably one of the most popular beaches in the area. It's a perfect example of a Caribbean beach with its clean, clear turquoise water and soft, sandy beach. It is the centerpiece of the Rainbow Bay Subdivision. The water is almost always calm and warm. Stop by this beach to swim, snorkel and just relax in the gently lapping waves of this Caribbean side beach.

Directions to access road - heading south

1.0 miles (1.6 kms) south of **Rainbow Inn** turn right onto Wandering Shore Drive. Watch for the road signs. The Rainbow Bay area is one of the few places you'll actually find street signs in Eleuthera.

Directions to access road - heading north

4.3 miles (6.9 kms) north of **James Cistern Pier** turn left onto Wandering Shore Drive.

Leave the highway at N 25° 20.188'~W 76° 26.033'

and continue for 0.25 miles (0.4 kms) to the Rainbow Bay Park Site parking area. The Rainbow Bay owners association has put aside several areas in the development for public use.

Access

This is an easy-access beach with paved road right to the beach and a designated parking area. Many of the roads in Rainbow Bay are paved. Take advantage of this easy-to-find beach to enjoy a relaxing ocean experience.

Privacy

There has always been someone else enjoying this beach whenever we have visited here and we do so frequently. But it has always been our experience that anyone we've met here has been friendly and welcoming. What better way to meet and make new friends?

Swimming

This is a particularly good swimming area. The bay has a clean, white sand bottom and it is shallow for a good distance out. The water is almost always calm, warm and welcoming.

Snorkeling

There is some good snorkeling around the larger rocks in the water and along the low cliffs. You'll find that some of the colorful fish will swim with you, but it has been our experience that groupers, although they may be nearby, like to hide.

Beachcombing

Shelling is generally good at this beach. Take your time and look around and you might come home with something special. We have been told that this is a good place to look for sand dollars.

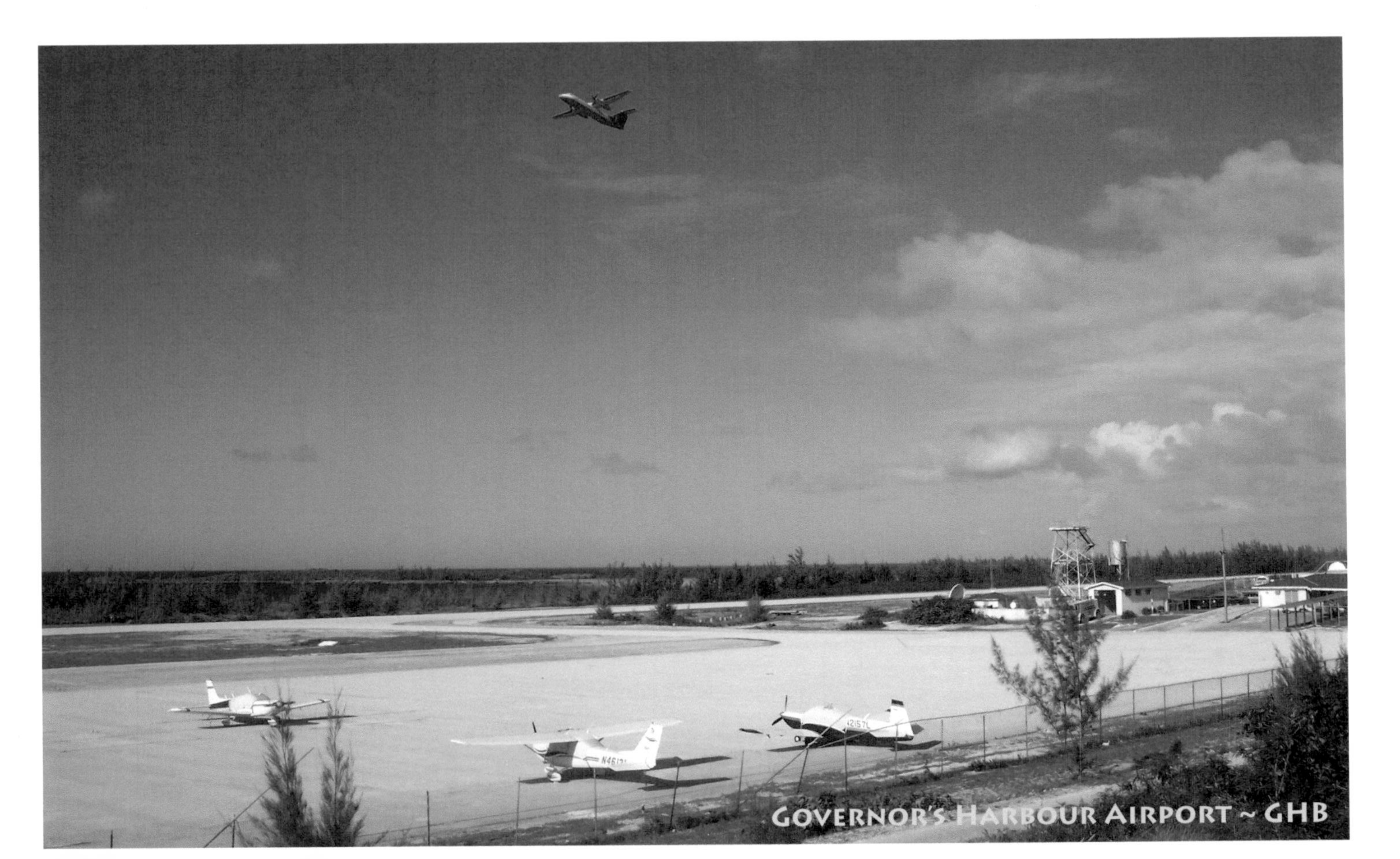
GOVERNOR'S HARBOUR AIRPORT ~ GHB

James Point Beach

N 25° 20.022'~W 76° 21.214'

REVISED: This is a long, wide beach that is certainly worth the visit. There is an old shipwreck, visible and easily accessible from the shore, just south of the entrance path to the beach. To the north is James Point. Getting there is quite a walk, but well worth the effort. If you take the time to make the walk, you'll be rewarded with a kind of "hot tub" formation carved, by the ocean waves, right into a large rock and yet another, smaller beach just beyond this point. This beach's beige sand is loosely packed, so for easier walking it would be best to stick closer to the shoreline where the sand is firmer and more compact.

Directions to access road - heading south

0.15 miles (0.2 kms) from **James Cistern Pier** turn left onto a paved road.

Directions to access road - heading north

6.4 miles (10.3 kms) from **Airport Liquor** turn right onto paved road.

Leave the highway at N 25° 19.503'~W 76° 21.735'

and go up the hill beside the **East and Final** grocery store. At the top of the hill take the gravel road forking off to the right. It is 0.8 miles (1.3 kms) to the beach from the Queen's Highway.

Access

This beach is easily accessible in a regular sedan, however, exercise some caution on the access road transitioning between the paved road and the gravel road. There's quite a dip. Also, the rest of the unpaved road can be bumpy in spots.

Privacy

You will frequently have this beach to yourself, but not always. We have encountered others at this beach on several occasions and there are always footprints in the sand. But it's a huge beach, so if you don't feel like socializing, you won't have to.

Swimming

As with most beaches on the Atlantic side, the waves and undertow can be strong. There are also quick drop-offs, so take care. We've been in the water here many times, but we always make sure we pick a calm day.

Snorkeling

We expected there to be some good snorkeling around the shipwreck but were disappointed, although others have had better luck. You might want to try around rocky areas but do it on very calm days.

Beachcombing

There's quite a few shells to be found, unfortunately many of them are broken. But, keep your eyes open, we have managed to come back from this beach with some really nice specimens. And, as this is an Atlantic side beach, you're likely to find all manner of items washed up here.

"WINNIE"
A TYPICAL POTCAKE

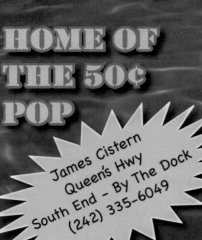

N 25° 19.693'~W 76° 22.434'

REVISED: This sometimes sandy, sometimes rocky Caribbean beach stretches the whole length of the James Cistern Settlement plus a good distance past. With little interruption it runs for about 2.5 miles (4 kms). There are some very nice spots and it is certainly easy to get to. Keep an eye out for a good spot to park. Our favorite spot is 2.4 mile (3.9 kms) north of **Airport Liquor** and 1.6 mile (2.6 kms) south of the **James Cistern Pier.**

The GPS reading given above is for the northern end of the beach, but be sure to explore all of it. Each section has its own treasures and charm. This is also a good place to purchase freshly caught fish at the concrete dock. Look for people selling their catches around 4pm each afternoon.

Directions to access road - heading south

There is no access road. It starts about 4.7 miles (7.6 kms) south of **Rainbow Inn**.

Directions to access road - heading north

There is no access road. It starts about 2.3 miles (3.7 Kms) north of **Airport Liquor**.

Leave the highway at N 25° 18.372'~W 76° 22.434'

As this entire beach is accessible directly from Queen's Highway, there are no directions for leaving the highway. The GPS reading given here is for the southern end of the beach.

Access

The entire length of this beach is accessible directly from Queen's Highway. Any car will do. But, while you're here, patronize some of the local shops and don't forget to stop by Blanche's fruit and vegetable stand.

Privacy

Don't expect any privacy here. The beach is quite popular in the settlement of James Cistern and the entire length of the beach is visible from Queen's Highway. But there's lots of beach to explore.

Swimming

Most of the length of this beach is good for swimming. It is calm, fairly shallow and has an even sandy bottom. The shoreline is broken up in spots by rocky sections followed by sandy sections and so on.

Snorkeling

There's good snorkeling around many of the rocky areas. Even on the Caribbean side, it's always best to swim or snorkel on calm days. If you choose to snorkel along here you will frequently be joined by some of the colorful fish that inhabit the waters here.

Beachcombing

Not a prime place for shelling but keep your eyes open, you might find that special one. We've also found other items on the beach, even someone's flipper.

James Cistern Pier

Sponge Cove

N 25° 18.060'~W 76° 20.152'

REVISED: The sand at this beach is beige and a bit coarse but it's still a nice protected cove. As long as the Corlas Village sign remains standing (and it's taken a beating over the last few years), finding this road is easy. When we first found this little cove we thought we had found a little piece of Heaven. It looked like something out of a movie set. However, on closer inspection we had to downgrade it just a little bit. But be sure to bring your camera. It's still a wonderful place to take photos, relax, paddle in the water and enjoy the view.

Directions to access road - heading south

2.7 miles (4.4 kms) south of **James Cistern Pier** turn left onto a semi-paved road. Look for the Corlas Village sign.

Directions to access road - heading north

2.7 miles (4.4 kms) north of **Airport Liquor** turn right onto a semi-paved road. Look for the Corlas Village sign.

Leave the highway at N 25° 17.719'~W 76° 20.335'

and continue for 0.6 miles (0.9 kms) directly to the beach.

Access

With extreme caution a regular sedan should be able to negotiate this road. There are a few rough spots and there is a deep trench on one side of the road. Be very careful. It would be easy to get a wheel stuck in that trench. And it wouldn't be very easy to extricate a car that did get stuck.

Privacy

We've seen footprints here but have never encountered anyone. It looks like efforts to further develop the subdivision are underway as there have been new roads cut. These things move slowly but development will most likely happen here.

Swimming

Even though this is the Atlantic side, the protected cove keeps the water fairly calm. There is, however, a fair bit of vegetation on the bottom and the water is not as clear as at other locations. However, depending on the wave action, the water can clear up.

Snorkeling

We tried snorkeling here but were disappointed. The water was murky and there was a lot of vegetation. We didn't see any fish. Perhaps it will be better when the water is clearer.

Beachcombing

There were a few shells but nothing spectacular. If you walk around the bay to the next straight section of beach you will find an area littered with Conch shells. Most of them are sun bleached but you might get lucky.

Transportation

Name / Phone No.	Website / Ports Served
Twin Air/Calypso from Fort Lauderdale	www.flytwinair.com
954-359-8266 (FL) 242-335-1696 (North Eleuthera) 242-332-3340 (Governor's Harbour) 242-334-2795 (Rock Sound)	North Eleuthera - ELH Governor's Harbour - GHB Rock Sound - RSD
Continental Connection from Miami and Fort Lauderdale	www.continental.com
954-688-7225 or 800-231-0856 (FL) 242-335-1278 (North Eleuthera) 242-332-3444 (Governor's Harbour)	North Eleuthera - ELH Governor's Harbour - GHB
Yellow Air Taxi from Fort Lauderdale	www.flyyellowairtaxi.com
1-800-yellow-4 954-359-0292 954-359-5324 (Fax)	North Eleuthera - ELH
Southern Air Charter from Nassau	www.southernaircharter.com
242-377-2014/5 (Nassau) 242-377-1066 (fax Nassau) 242-335-1720 (Governor's Harbour) 242-354-2035 (North Eleuthera)	North Eleuthera - ELH Governor's Harbour - GHB
Bahamas Air from Nassau	www.bahamasair.com
242-377-8451 (Nassau) 242-377-7409 (fax - Nassau) 242-335-1152 (North Eleuthera) 242-332-2648 (Governor's Harbour) 242-334-2125 (Rock Sound)	North Eleuthera - ELH Governor's Harbour - GHB Rock Sound - RSD
Lynx Air from Fort Lauderdale	www.lynxair.com
888-596-9247 (FL Reservations) 954-772-9808 (FL) 954-772-1141 (fax)	Governor's Harbour - GHB
Bo Hengy fast ferry from Nassau	www.bahamasferries.com
242-323-2166 or 242-323-2165 (Nassau) 242-323-8185 or 242-394-8457 (fax Nassau)	Spanish Wells Harbour Island Governor's Harbour
Mail Boat from Nassau	
242-393-1064 (Nassau)	All Islands

Airport Beach ~ North

N 25° 17.950'~W 76° 19.944'

REVISED: This wide, pink sand beach drops off into the water in "steps". There is an undertow even on calm days. The sand is soft, powdery and pink. This is just the beginning of a long, long beach, which is why we have devoted several pages to this fabulous beach so we could document each of the access points and the differences between each section. Keeping reading on to the next few pages to get a more expanded description and feel for the entire beach. This is one of our favorite beaches (all of it) and we visit here often.

Directions to access road - heading south

3.0 miles (4.8 kms) south of **James Cistern Pier** turn left onto a gravel road.

Directions to access road - heading north

1.1 miles (1.8 kms) north of **Airport Liquor** turn right onto a gravel road.

Leave the highway at N 25° 17.589'~W 76° 20.130'

and continue for a total of 0.6 miles (0.95 kms) to the beach, turning left at 0.25 miles (0.4 kms), right at 0.3 miles (0.5 kms), left again at 0.4 miles (0.6 kms) and right again at 0.55 miles (0.9 kms). At this last turn you'll find a short sandy road that goes right to the beach.

Access

This recently cleared road is accessible by any car with reasonable caution. So take it easy you'll be fine. Be on the lookout for a wooden garbage holder at the entrance to the road.

Privacy

At the beginning of airport beach there are a few houses overlooking the beach. Even though we have never encountered anyone, there have always been footprints in the sand.

Swimming

We wouldn't recommend swimming here. There are steep drop-offs and a very strong undertow. We usually just content ourselves with a long walk and paddling in the water close to shore.

Snorkeling

Because we wouldn't recommend swimming here, neither do we recommend snorkeling. There are lots of other places to snorkel where it much nicer and much safer, so why ruin your day?

Beachcombing

We didn't find any shells worth mentioning on this portion of Airport Beach. But you can frequently find something unusual washed up on an Atlantic side beach.

Airport Beach ~ Center

N 25° 16.638'~W 76° 19.106'

REVISED: The beautiful pink sand here rivals Lighthouse beach. The beach is cool, soft and firm making it great for those long, leisurely romantic strolls. To the south you can see the remains of the US Naval base and the damage that was done by hurricane Andrew. The military has long since left, but you can find some nostalgic websites about servicemen's days in Eleuthera.

Directions to access road - heading south

0.4 miles (0.7 kms) south of **Airport Liquor** turn left onto a dirt road. Go slowly, this road is easy to miss. Since our first publication another road had been cut just to the North of this one. We believe access on that road is restricted.

Directions to access road - heading north

7.4 miles (11.9 kms) north of the **Duck Inn** turn right onto a dirt road. Go slowly, this road is easy to miss. Since our first publication another road had been cut just to the North of this one. We believe access on that road is restricted

Leave the highway at N 25° 16.457'~W 76° 19.267'

and go just 0.2 miles (0.35 kms) to a parking area on top of the dune. Walk down the path to the beach where steps have been built out of driftwood and old milk crates.

Access

By exercising reasonable caution you can take any car to this beach, but it's really just a dirt track. Be careful, this road ends at a sandy cliff so don't go too far. If your car lands on the beach - well - you've gone too far.

Privacy

Although we have always seen footprints on this beach we have never run into anyone else here and this is one of our favorite beaches. It would depend on how many other people got the urge to visit this beach on the same day.

Swimming

It is relatively calm here for the Atlantic side but we have encountered waves that have knocked us to the ground on more than one occasion. (Don't you hate it when that happens!)

Snorkeling

You may want to try snorkeling on calm days around some of the rocky areas but we didn't find it worthwhile. We prefer to just play in the surf, walk on the beach and enjoy the scenery.

Beachcombing

We have found very few shells on this beach but there are other beachcombing items that get washed up on shore. You may find some of them interesting.

Airport Beach ~ South

N 25° 15.637'~W 76° 18.060'

Like the rest of Airport Beach, the sand is soft, cool and pink. The sand along the shoreline is firm, making this a good walking beach. This is the southern-most end of a very, very long beach. If you feel adventurous, you may want to try walking the entire length of this fabulous beach. Take lots of water, a few snacks and your camera. It may take you quite a while to walk the entire beach. Particularly if you make stops along the way to rest, swim, look for shells, do some beachcombing, watch the waves, take pictures and just enjoy the day. If this is your plan, you best plan to spend the entire day here.

Directions to access road - heading south

2.2 miles (3.5 kms) south of **Airport Liquor** turn left onto Knowles Drive into the Breeze-Away Subdivision.

Directions to access road - heading north

5.7 miles (9.1 kms) north of the **Duck Inn** turn right onto Knowles Drive into the Breeze-Away Subdivision.

Leave the highway at N 25° 15.292'~W 76° 18.206'

and proceed for 0.4 miles (0.6 kms) to the end of Knowles Drive directly to the beach.

Access

This access to the southern part of Airport beach, by way of Knowles Road in the Breeze-Away Subdivision, gives you paved road right to the beach. Any car can make this trip.

Privacy

Although there are not many houses in this subdivision, yet, there are some on the beach. We have never encountered anyone else on this beach but there's always lots of footprints, so don't count on any privacy.

Swimming

Swimming is good as it remains fairly shallow close to shore, but remember it's the Atlantic side and there can be some pretty good waves from time to time, so always pick a calm day.

Snorkeling

There may be some good snorkeling around the rocky area at the end of the road but we have never been here when it was calm enough to try. We don't recommend you snorkel here unless it is very calm.

Beachcombing

We didn't find a lot of shells on this beach, but take the time to look around. You never know when the one gem might be peeking out of the sand.

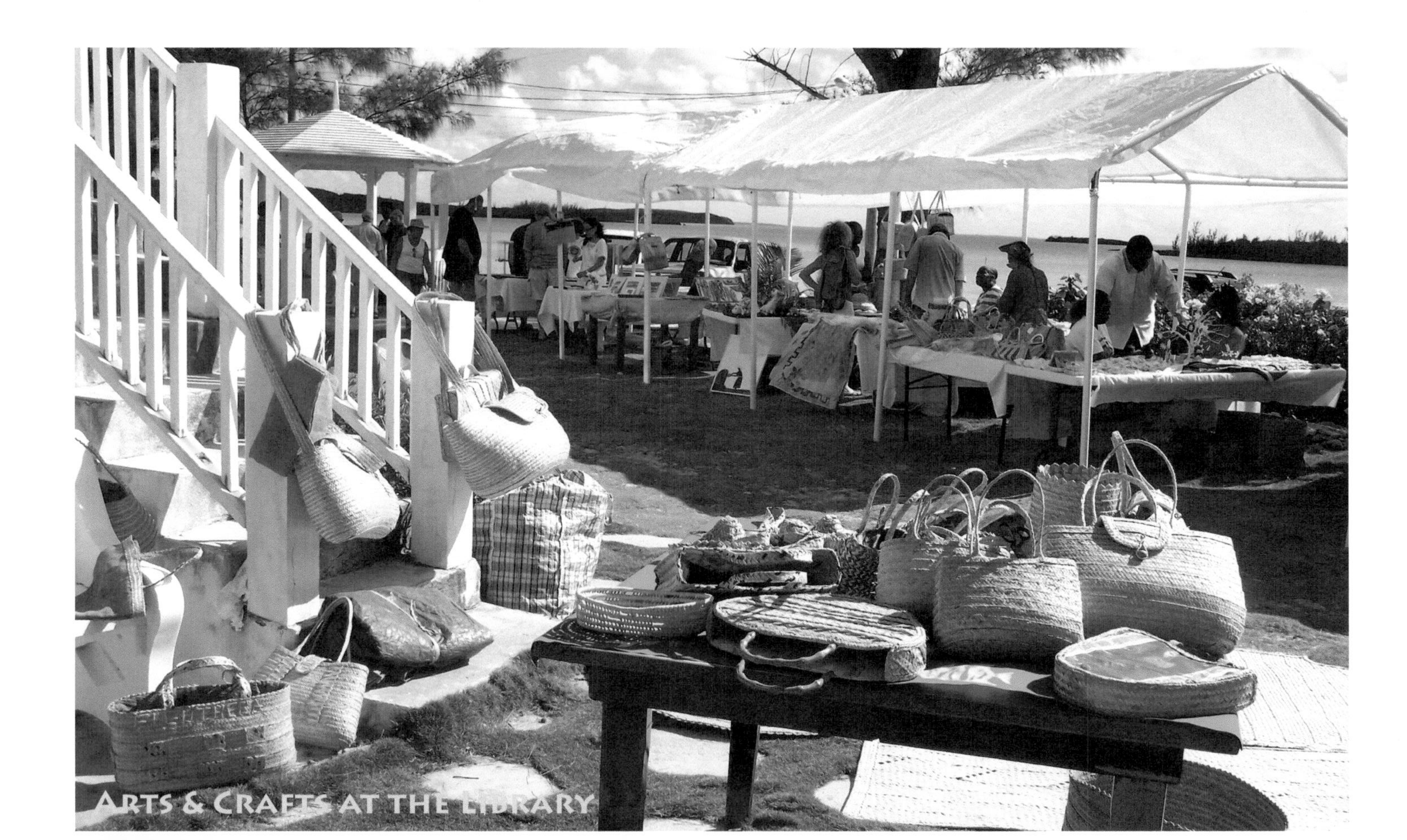

Arts & Crafts at the Library

N 25° 15.822'~W 76° 19.067'

REVISED: Also known as Receiver's Beach (from the US military days), this long, curving beach has powdery white sand and extends for more than a mile from the south end of the Governor's Harbour airport (GHB). As it is on the Caribbean side of the island, the water is usually calm and warm. It is also very shallow for a good distance out. It's an excellent picnic spot, with many trees for shade, so bring along some snacks and drinks and plan to spend the day. In the previous edition we mentioned that a new resort was being built on this beach. The Cocodimama Charming Resort has since been completed and boasts three colorful buildings with hotel rooms and a restaurant as well. You are also close to **Airport Liquor** where you can get a cold drink and light snacks.

Directions to access road - heading south

1.1 miles (1.8 kms) south of **Airport Liquor** turn right at the paved road.

Directions to access road - heading north

6.7 miles (10.8 kms) north of the **Duck Inn** turn left at the paved road.

Leave the highway at N 25° 15.915'~W 76° 18.980'

and proceed for 0.1 miles (0.2 kms) on the paved road right to the beach. Look for the colorful buildings of the **Cocodimama Charming Resort** on your right.

Access

This easily accessible beach has paved road right to the beach. Look for a spot to park under the palm and pine trees while taking some time to enjoy the beach and the calm Caribbean water.

Privacy

This is a popular spot and now that the new resort has been finished, it is even more popular with both local visitors and guests from the resort. It is also visible from the Queen's Highway so don't expect any privacy.

Swimming

The bottom is clean and sandy and the water is calm and shallow making this a great place to go swimming. The waves are often small and rolling but can become a bit rough when the wind kicks up.

Snorkeling

Check out the snorkeling around the rocky areas at the tip of the point. You may get to see some of the colorful fish and they may even swim with you. We have found, though, that the tasty fish - like grouper - tend to hide.

Beachcombing

In the last edition we reported that this was not a very good shelling beach. However, upon subsequent visits we have found a lot of very nice, intact shells.

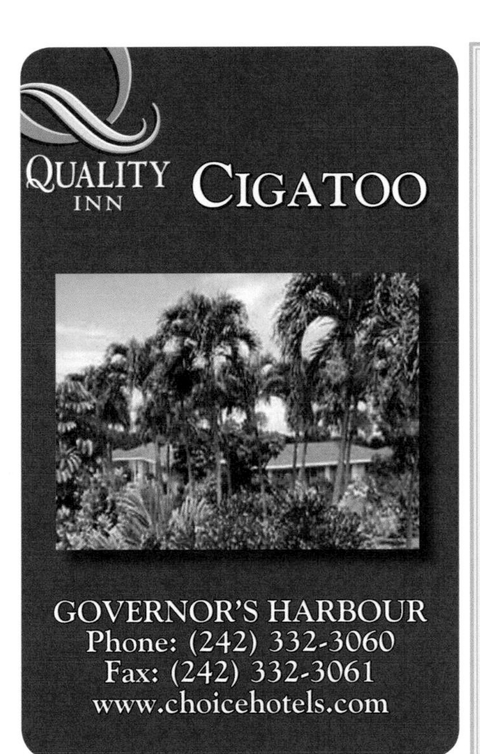

QUALITY
INN
CIGATOO
GOVERNOR'S HARBOUR
Phone: (242) 332-3060
Fax: (242) 332-3061
www.choicehotels.com

Fast Facts

Eleuthera's population (including Harbour Island and Spanish Wells) as of the 1990 census – 10,524

Eleuthera has a total area of 200 sq. miles and its highest point is 168 ft. above sea level.

National bird

Flamingo

National fish

Blue marlin

National flower

Yellow elder (*Tecoma stans* or *Stenolobium stans*)

National tree

Lignum vitae "Tree of life" (*Guaiacum sanctum*)

Twin Cove Beach

N 25° 12.829'~W 76° 14.653'

Bring your camera and your snorkel gear to this beach. These beautiful Twin Coves (hence the name) are lined with mature palm trees and boast clear blue water. It's a pleasant spot for some swimming, snorkeling and relaxing. You can continue south on the sandy road to find even more beaches, but the road gets rougher as you travel south.

Directions to access road - heading south

6.5 miles (10.4 kms) south of **Airport Liquor** go left onto a paved road (just south of the Worker's Complex).

Directions to access road - heading north

1.4 miles (2.2 kms) north of the **Duck Inn** turn right onto a paved road.

Leave the highway at N 25° 12.660'~W 76° 15.331'

and continue along this road for a total of 0.9 miles (1.4 kms). This road will take a 90 deg bend to the right and then another to the left, bringing you to a T-junction at a dirt road at 0.6 miles (1.0 kms). Turn right on this dirt road and continue for 0.25 miles (0.4 kms) past a house on your left, to a small parking area. (You can't see the house from the parking area.)

Access

Initially you'll be travelling on paved road, but watch out for some potholes. The sandy road is fairly smooth. Any car can negotiate this road with reasonable care. The road does get rougher as you continue south past this beach, though.

Privacy

There is a house on the northern cove (don't you just wish it was yours?) and we've always seen footprints in the sand. Even though we have never encountered anyone on our visits, don't plan on a lot of privacy.

Swimming

With two coves to swim in how can you go wrong? Take your pick and go for a plunge. The swimming is great in these well protected coves. As always, though, with an Atlantic side beach, pick a calm day to go swimming.

Snorkeling

Be sure to bring your snorkel gear and check out the rocky areas. We're sure you'll have a good time looking for colorful fish and, perhaps, the odd starfish. But, remember this is the Atlantic side and pick a calm day.

Beachcombing

We didn't find a lot of shells but things change on a daily basis. Look around and you might stumble across an unexpected treasure.

N 25° 11.543'~W 76° 14.814'

Governor's Harbour and Anchor Bay beach are separated only by the causeway to Cupid's Cay. You'll see many ocean-going vessels come into the government dock in Governor's Harbour as well as the Bo Hengy hydrofoil on Fridays and Sundays. Anchor Bay is the site of a fish fry every Friday night. These beaches are an easy walk from **The Duck Inn** and downtown Governor's Harbour. Frequently you can purchase freshly caught fish (and lobster in season) from the local fishermen. Check out the concrete boat ramp at the main intersection (there was a traffic light but it's not working right now) in the afternoons to see what's available.

Directions to access road - heading south

Parliament Drive is right across the Queen's Highway from the **Duck Inn**.

Directions to access road - heading north

19.6 miles (31.6 kms) north of **Ingraham's Beach Inn** turn left onto Parliament Drive.

Leave the highway at N 25° 12.660'~W 76° 15.331'

and proceed along Parliament Drive for 0.3 miles (0.5 kms) and the beaches are on either side of the causeway leading to Cupid's Cay.

Access

As these beaches are in the heart of Governor's Harbour, access couldn't be easier. Any car will do. You can even park your car some distance away and do a walking tour as well as visit the beaches.

Privacy

Don't expect any privacy while enjoying these beaches. As mentioned earlier, they are both in the center of Governor's Harbour. But you can still enjoy the beaches and get some great pictures, too.

Swimming

Anchor Bay is a great place to enjoy a leisurely swim and the Governor's Harbour side has lots of beach area at low tide. There are frequently small boats anchored in the bay making a terrific photo opportunity.

Snorkeling

Try Anchor Bay for snorkeling. There are lots of places in this bay where small fish can hide. You'll see coral and other sea creatures, as well. You could easily float around for a long time and enjoy watching some underwater occupants.

Beachcombing

There's lots of shells here but you'll have to look carefully to find some prime specimens. We also found a lot of sea glass along the rockier sections - some of them quite unusual.

Damianos | Sotheby's
INTERNATIONAL REALTY

www.SIRbahamas.com

SPANISH WELLS, ELEUTHERA #3600
Luxury 3 bedroom 3 bath home on North Side Beach. Fabulous views, 1.25-acre lot. **$4,950,000.**
Darrin.Sands@SothebysRealty.com
+1.242.557.7071 www.SIRbahamas.com

CURRENT, ELEUTHERA #3611 Pristine half-acre beachfront lot located in quaint village. Amazing sea views, good potential. **$475,000.**
Virginia.Damianos@SothebysRealty.com
+1.242.322.2305 www.SIRbahamas.com

Rainbow Bay Aerial

RAINBOW BAY, ELEUTHERA Two adjacent lots with over 175 feet of waterfront. North of the Governor's Harbour Airport. **$310,000.**
Jonathan.P.Morris@SothebysRealty.com
+1.242.332.2820 www.SIRbahamas.com

N. PALMETTO POINT, ELEUTHERA #3182
Immaculate 2 bed 2 bath beach house on 3/4-acre with sweeping ocean views. **US$725,000.**
Jonathan.P.Morris@SothebysRealty.com
+1.242.332.2820 www.SIRbahamas.com

DOUBLE BAY, ELEUTHERA #3412
Beachfront 1.5-acre parcel with 150 feet of pink sand beach and 441 feet deep. **US$975,000.**
Virginia.Damianos@SothebysRealty.com
+1.242.322.2305 www.SIRbahamas.com

COTTON BAY, ELEUTHERA #2536 Exclusive 1,500-acre private resort community. Ocean view lots from **$650,000.** Beachfront lots from **$1.0M.**
Virginia.Damianos@SothebysRealty.com
+1.242.322.2305 www.SIRbahamas.com

DAMIANOS SOTHEBY'S INTERNATIONAL REALTY, t +1.242.322.2305 info.Bahamas@SothebysRealty.com

French Leave Beach

N 25° 11.911'~W 76° 13.709'

REVISED: This beach, also known as Club Med Beach, was the location of a Club Med Resort until Hurricane Floyd did major damage to the resort in 1999. The new French Leave resort is currently being built on this property. We don't yet know what the policy will be for non-residents to access the beach from the resort but there are two short roads (see access directions) just past the Club's entrance. This wide, pink sand beach is flat and firm, just right for a long stroll.

Directions to access road - heading south

Turn left at the **Duck Inn** onto Lignum Vitae which is the right hand road going up the hill at the lights.

Directions to access road - heading north

19.6 miles (31.6 kms) north of **Ingraham's Beach Inn** turn right onto Lignum Vitae at the Governor's Harbour lights.

Leave the highway at N 25° 12.660'~W 76° 15.331'

and continue up the hill. Turn right on Coconut Palm Drive, which becomes North-shore Drive after passing the **Cigatoo Resort**. At 1.0 miles (1.7 kms) turn left onto a sandy track. The beach is just 200 ft. in. Continue past this road for another 0.2 miles (0.35 kms) to find another sandy access road to this beach.

Access

The French Leave Beach is easily accessible. It is mostly paved road with short sandy roads, at the north and south ends, taking you directly to the beach. So any car can make it to this beach.

Privacy

This is a popular beach and there are several houses along the shoreline, as well. Don't expect any privacy here. But don't let that stop you from visiting. This is a fabulous beach - bring your camera!

Swimming

Even though this is an Atlantic side beach, the water stays fairly calm, the bottom is sandy and it remains shallow for a good distance out. Go ahead and enjoy a day, or more, of swimming at this beach.

Snorkeling

For snorkeling, check out the rocky areas at the north and south ends of the beach. But, remember, pick a calm day to get the most enjoyment out of your snorkeling experi-ence.

Beachcombing

As with most reef protected beaches, you won't find a lot of shells. We did find a few small specimens, but nothing that we felt was worth taking home to our shell garden.

Papaw Bay

N26° 09.044' ~ W76° 11.335'

We had driven by the Papaw Beach street sign many times before we actually decided to explore down this road. We're certainly glad we did! It leads to a lovely beach with a small cay just offshore. Being a Caribbean side beach, the water is shallow in most places and relatively calm most of the time. But, as we frequently suggest, check the weather. Even the calmest water can become choppy if the weather gets rough. But this is a terrific beach to spend some time just walking the beach and playing in the water.

Directions to access road - heading south

0.65 miles (1.05 kms) north of **Island Farms & Nursery** turn left onto the Papaw Bay road.

Directions to access road - heading north

4.85 miles (7.8 kms) south of the **Duck Inn**, turn right onto the Papaw Bay road.

Leave the highway at N 25° 33.481'~W 76° 41.757'

and travel 0.6 miles (0.96 kms) and take the road on your right. Then travel 0.1 miles (0.16 kms), the road bends to the right but pull straight ahead just past that road and park. The beach is just a few steps in front of you.

Access

This appears to be a fairly well traveled road. You'll pass some farming and some construction on the way to the beach. Just watch for a couple of rough spots and any car can make it to this beach.

Privacy

Like many of Eleuthera's beaches your privacy will vary with the time of year. Although we have never encountered anyone else on our visits to this beach, there are two or three private residences on the shoreline and we often saw footprints in the sand. Expect more privacy in the summer than the winter.

Swimming

We have enjoyed swimming here many times. We tried reaching the cay that is just offshore, but found it got too deep for us. A good swimmer may be able to swim out to the cay, which seems to have its own beach as well.

Snorkeling

We didn't have our snorkel gear with us when we visited this beach, but we would have liked to snorkel around the little cay just offshore. If you get a chance to snorkel here, drop us a line and let us know what you found.

Beachcombing

We found a few shells at this beach, but nothing that we felt was worth taking home with us. As mentioned many times, though, the number of shells on a beach can change on an almost daily basis.

Photo courtesy of DolceVita

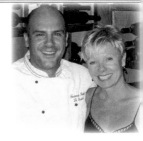

N 25° 08.960'~W 76° 10.972'

Palmetto Point has a typical Caribbean side beach. The sand is soft and powdery, the water is shallow, calm and clear and the bottom is even and sandy. There is a concrete dock and a couple of palapas on the beach. There are frequently events going on at this beach. You may want to join in on some of the festivities hosted here. Take the time to check out Palmetto Point's website for information about any upcoming events - *www.palmettopoint.org*

Directions to access road - heading south

5.0 miles (8.1 kms) south of the **Duck Inn** turn right onto Seaview Drive (Church Street on the Atlantic side).

Directions to access road - heading north

14.7 miles (23.6 kms) north of **Ingraham's Beach Inn** turn left onto Seaview Drive (Church Street on the Atlantic side).

Leave the highway at N 25° 09.419'~W 76° 10.808'

and go 0.5 miles (0.8 kms) to the beach. You'll pass Shore Drive at 0.4 miles (0.6 kms) which is the road to RunAway bay and the DolceVita restaurant. It's just 1.1 miles (1.8 kms) down a paved road. The food is great and the owners are friendly - what more can you ask.

Access

This beach is easily accessible by any car as there is paved road all the way. Just a reminder to always drive on the left side. We find that it's when we make turns that we often end up on the wrong (right-hand) side of the road.

Privacy

As this beach is in the settlement of South Palmetto Point you won't find any privacy here. But you may want to take advantage of some of the events that are hosted at this beach.

Swimming

Calm, clear waters and an even sandy bottom make for a good swimming experience. The waves can kick up some of the time, depending on the weather. But, if you've got a nice calm day then the swimming should be good.

Snorkeling

Check out the rocks on either side of this small bay for some good snorkeling. There are some fish that actually seem to like to swim with snorkelers. So look around and enjoy the underwater view.

Beachcombing

We didn't find a lot of shells on the beach but you might find some while snorkeling. Please don't take any shells that are still occupied.

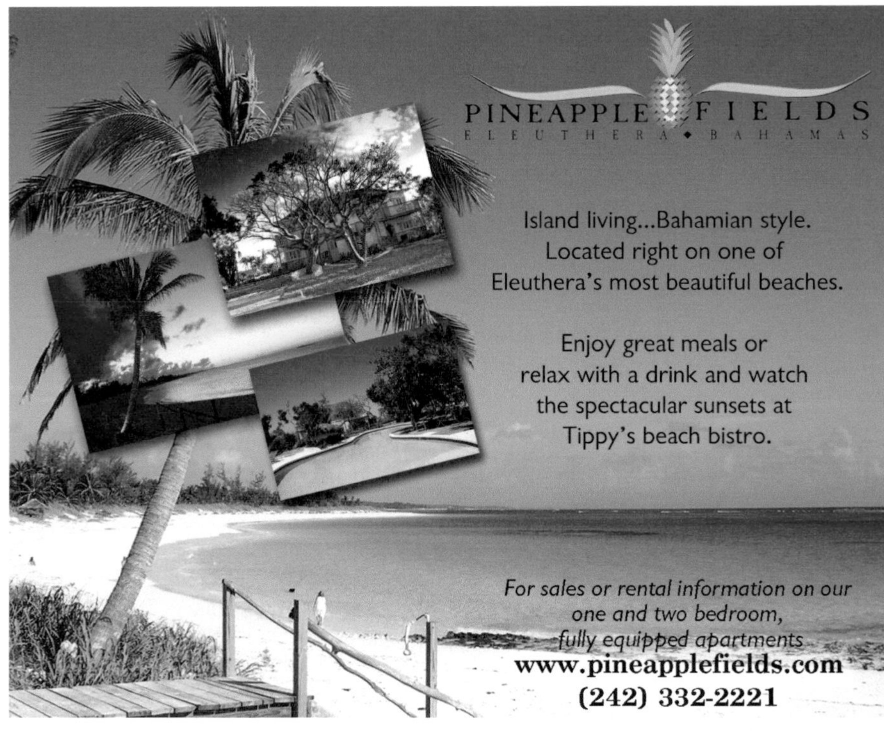

Pineapple Fields and Conch'd Out are located on a beach that winds all the way from French Leave (formerly Club Med Beach) to Double Bay in a pretty much unbroken stretch of sand. And, along this desirable stretch of beach you'll find many incredible houses.

Because of the number of homes and estates it is difficult to find a public access point to the beach. But be sure to check out the directions given on several pages in this book. And, please, always remember to respect private property. There are still several ways to access this fabulous beach without trespassing.

One access point is from Tippy's Restaurant, just across from Pineapple Fields. We've been told that you can find some good snorkeling just off the beach at Tippy's. There are some reefs within easy reach of the shore. If you're lucky, you could encounter lobsters, rays and sea turtles, not to mention lots of other colorful native ocean dwellers.

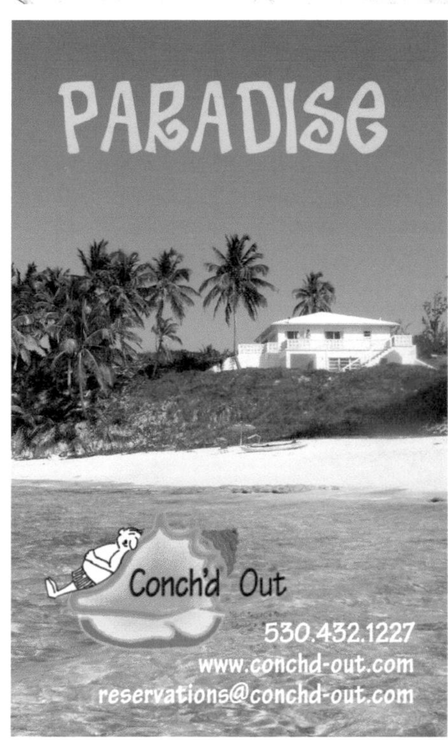

Poponi Beach

N 25° 10.215'~W 76° 10.256'

This beach is very similar, if a bit smaller, to the Unique Village beach. It has wonderfully soft pink sand and is reef-protected. It is also very close to Unique Village itself. You'll pass the access road to this beach just before you get to the Unique Village road. This beach boasts lots of palm and pine trees, so there's shade when you need it. It's certainly worth a look while you're out exploring all the terrific beaches this area has to offer.

Directions to access road - heading south

4.9 miles (7.9 kms) south of **Duck Inn** turn left onto Church Street.

Directions to access road - heading north

14.7 miles (23.6 kms) north of **Ingraham's Beach Inn**. Turn right onto Church Street.

Leave the highway at N 25° 09.419'~W 76° 10.808'

and proceed for 0.8 miles (1.3 kms) east on Church Street. Church Street (Seaview Drive) is the main intersection in Palmetto Point. At the T-junction (Northshore Drive). Turn right and go 0.3 miles (0.55 kms) and turn left onto a dirt road. Continue on the dirt road for 0.1 miles (0.2 kms) to a parking area at the beach.

Access

Access to this beach is mostly by paved road, with a short section of dirt track. That makes this beach easily accessible by any car. Just be careful when you leave the paved road. Take it slowly and you'll be fine.

Privacy

There are two houses on this beach, so don't expect a lot of privacy. We haven't encountered any people when we've stopped at this beach but we're sure the homeowners use this beach whenever they can.

Swimming

Even though this beach is on the Atlantic side, the water remains fairly calm. So go ahead, jump in and enjoy a swim. But, as we always caution, pick a calm day. This is the Atlantic side and the waves can kick up.

Snorkeling

Check out the snorkeling around the rocky areas and coral heads. Just be sure to do your snorkeling on calm days so you get the best experience. Safety is always a good idea.

Beachcombing

We didn't find a lot of shells at this beach, but if you're into beachcombing there were a lot of interesting items washed up here.

Unique Village

N 25° 10.115'~W 76° 10.015'

This long pink sand beach is great for strolling, swimming or snorkeling. It rivals the beach at Harbour Island, but without the crowds. Although "crowds" in Eleuthera is a relative term, even on Harbour Island. But here's your chance to experience a true pink sand beach and have it mostly to yourselves. Bring your camera - the view is fantastic. There is a good restaurant in Unique Village making this a great place to stop for a while.

Directions to access road - heading south

5.0 miles (8.0 kms) south of **Duck Inn** turn left onto Church Street.

Directions to access road - heading north

14.7 miles (23.6 kms) north of **Ingraham's Beach Inn**. Turn right onto Church Street.

Leave the highway at N 25° 09.419'~W 76° 10.808'

and proceed for 0.8 miles (1.3 kms) east on Church Street. Church Street (Seaview Drive) is the main intersection in Palmetto Point. At the T-junction (Northshore Drive). Turn right and go 0.5 miles (0.9 kms) to Resorts Drive - turn left, continue for 0.1 miles (0.2 kms), and you're there.

Access

There are good roads right to the **Unique Village** resort. Watch for a few pot holes on the road in. A stairway in front of the Unique Village restaurant gives easy access to the beach.

Privacy

As this beach is at a resort it is likely you will not be alone. There are several rental units here - apartments, villas, small houses. It will depend on the time of year how many people you might encounter on this beach.

Swimming

It's like Harbour Island but without the crowds. Go ahead and enjoy a day of swimming on this relatively calm, reef-protected beach. As we always suggest, go an a calm day. Even though this beach is reef-protected it is still on the Atlantic side.

Snorkeling

Bring your snorkel gear and check out the rocky areas. But, be sure to do your snorkeling on a calm day. Some pretty impressive waves can kick up here depending on the weather and the wind.

Beachcombing

Check around, you can often find nice specimens on the Atlantic side.

BAHAMAS CASTAWAY
at Double Bay
www.bahamascastaway.com

COURTESY OF BAHAMAS CASTAWAY

Double Bay

N 25° 07.575'~W 76° 07.227'

This long powdery soft pink sand beach has many houses along it's length - some are estates and quite spectacular. Some of these houses are owned by winter residents and even the odd celebrity. Others are available for rent. After driving by all these wonderful places, we found a good access point at the very end of the road that runs parallel to the beach. There is a place to park and palm trees for shade. The sand is firm and good for taking those long walks. Don't forget your camera. An underwater camera would be a plus as well.

Directions to access road - heading south

8.0 miles (12.8 kms) south of **Duck Inn** turn left at the paved access road.

Directions to access road - heading north

11.6 miles (18.7 kms) north of **Ingraham's Beach Inn** turn right at the paved access road.

Leave the highway at N 25° 07.802'~W 76° 08.699'

and proceed on this paved road for 1.0 miles (1.6 kms) to a gravel road. Turn right and proceed for approximately 1.0 miles (1.7 kms) then take the sand road on your left for 0.1 miles (0.2 kms) directly to the beach.

Access

With a combination of paved roads and firm sand tracks, any car can easily make it to this beach. Just take it slow in some spots and keep your eyes open for pot holes and the like.

Privacy

There are many fabulous houses along this beach so don't expect much privacy but there are no buildings yet at the access point we have described. As always, please respect people's private property.

Swimming

There are waves - this is the Atlantic side, after all - but it is fairly shallow for quite a way out. We didn't experience any undertow at this portion of the beach. But always be careful.

Snorkeling

There's some good snorkeling around the rocks at the southern end of the beach close to the access point. There is also snorkeling at the reef. Again, be sure to pick a calm day. You'll probably need a boat if you're going to check out the reef.

Beachcombing

We didn't find a lot of shells here but there's always the chance of a serendipitous find.

Eleuthera-Vacations.com

N 25° 07.259'~W 76° 09.048'

This wide, sandy beach sits in a protected bay on the Caribbean side of Eleuthera. There is plenty of room to park your car and you'll find some shade provided by the numerous palm trees dotting the shoreline. Ten Bay would be a good place to not only have a picnic, but to swim and do a bit of snorkeling as well. It's a relatively easy beach to find and well worth the effort to find it. Make the time to check this beach out and you won't be disappointed. If you're time on the island is limited, you might want to check out Double Bay, on the Atlantic side, on the same day, as they are pretty close together. But, don't rush yourselves at either beach because they're both worth spending time at.

Directions to access road - heading south

9.2 miles (14.8 kms) south of **Duck Inn** turn right at a dirt road.

Directions to access road - heading north

10.4 miles (16.7 kms) north of **Ingraham's Beach Inn** turn left at a dirt road.

Leave the highway at N 25° 07.248'~W 76° 08.677'

and proceed for 0.4 miles (0.7 kms) towards the Caribbean side. There is a large, very old, A-frame type house on the corner of this access road that has seen better days.

Access

The access road to Ten Bay Beach is negotiable by pretty much any car. There are a few bumpy areas along the first bit of the road and then it gets sandy as you get closer to the beach.

Privacy

There are several houses overlooking this well protected bay, so don't expect any privacy at this beach. You will probably still feel like you have the beach to yourselves, though.

Swimming

This calm protected bay has a clean sandy bottom and is shallow for a good distance out. If you decide to go for a swim at this beach we're sure you'll enjoy yourselves. It's normally calm, but even the Caribbean side can get rough from time to time.

Snorkeling

Try snorkeling at either end of the bay where it is rocky and some small cliffs overhang the water. You're likely to get a glimpse of some resident sea life. If you've got an underwater camera, bring it along.

Beachcombing

We didn't find many shells here but we have been told it is a good place to search for sand dollars.

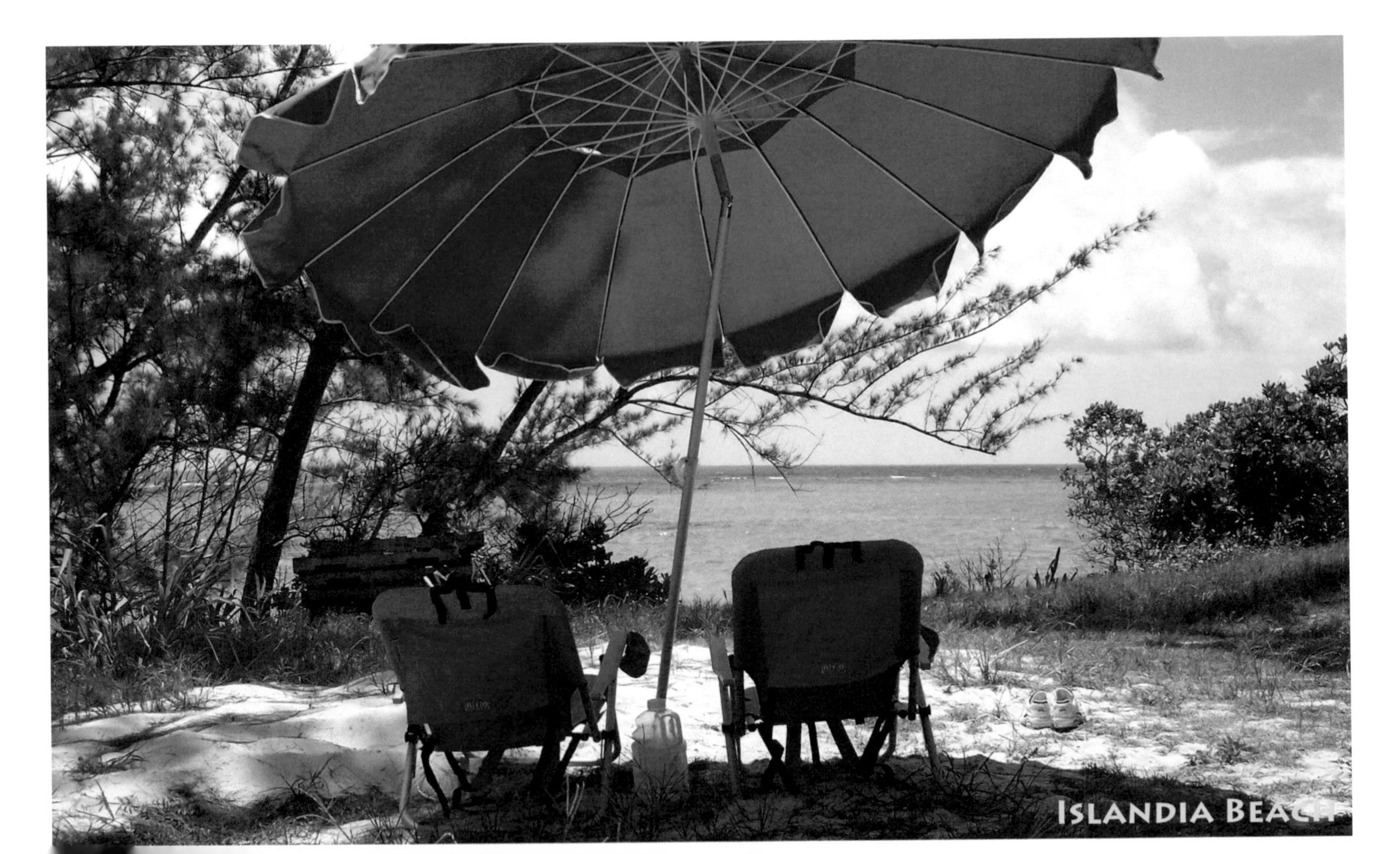

ISLANDIA BEACH

Islandia Beach

N25° 00.446' ~ W76° 07.921'

NEW: This long, wide Atlantic side beach can be a little difficult to find. It has soft white sand and seems to stretch on forever both north and south of the access point. If you miss this access road, there's another new road to the south. The next access road has been cut for a new subdivision and is very wide and easy to negotiate. However, the last time we were there, the road didn't lead directly to the beach, but it was just a short walk from where it ended. Also, if you choose the subdivision road, don't expect much privacy on the beach and we don't yet know if visitors will be welcome.

Directions to access road - heading south

16.25 miles (26.15 kms) south of **The Duck Inn**, turn left onto an overgrown road. (Note: there is a concrete post on the North side of the access road)

Directions to access road - heading north

2.3 miles (3.7 kms) North of the **Ingraham's Beach Inn**, turn right onto an overgrown road. (Note: there is a concrete post on the North side of the access road)

Leave the highway at N 25° 00.310'~W 76° 08.673'

and proceed for 0.75 miles (1.2 kms) and turn left and proceed for 0.09 miles (0.15 kms) to a clearing where you can park your car. The beach will be right in front of you. The photo on the left is taken at the parking area.

Access

The road was previously paved, but is now cracked and broken - but fairly even, so any car can make it without losing the oil pan. However, it is also pretty overgrown, so there is a real good chance you're car will get scratched by bushes on either side of the road.

Privacy

This access is fairly difficult to find, so odds are good you'll have the beach all to yourselves when you visit here.

Swimming

This is an Atlantic side beach, so you may encounter some large waves. However, this beach is also reef protected, so you don't get really deep water right from the shore and often the Atlantic waves are dampened.

Snorkeling

Unfortunately we haven't tried snorkeling here yet. If you try it, just look to the weather and the condition of the ocean.

Beachcombing

We found a few interesting shells here and a fair bit of other items washed onshore, such as nets, buoys and bottles.

Savannah Sound Beach

N 25° 05.667'~W 76° 07.777'

The drive along this long, narrow, sandy beach, going north from the settlement, is quite interesting. You'll find a few places to stop and enjoy both the scenery and the beach. And, you'll pass some very impressive houses in locations you'd least expect. The road, unfortunately, doesn't go anywhere, so you'll have to turn around and come back the way you came. You'll find several shady spots to park the car that are perfect for a romantic picnic.

Directions to access road - heading south

11.0 miles (9.8 kms) south of **Duck Inn** Turn left onto a paved road blasted through the cut.

Directions to access road - heading north

8.6 miles (13.8 kms) north of the **Ingraham's Beach Inn**. Turn right onto paved road through blasted cut.

Leave the highway at N 25° 05.246'~W 76° 07.993'

and proceed for 0.3 miles (0.5 kms) along paved road that runs through a blasted cut with very high, straight sides. This road will take you directly to the beach and the sand road that runs north, parallel to the beach.

Access

There is easy access to this beach by either paved roads or flat, firm sand roads. Any car can make it along this stretch. Just be on the look out for pot holes or bumps and dips in the road.

Privacy

If you take the sand road along the shore going north you're likely to find some secluded spots. The further you go north along the sand road, the more likely you'll have the beach to yourselves.

Swimming

Because this beach is sheltered, for the most part, by Windermere Island, it is calm most of the time. It is fairly shallow with an even sandy bottom. Always look to the weather, though, and remember this is still the Atlantic side.

Snorkeling

There's some snorkeling around the rocky areas, of which there are several. With such a long beach there are many sites that might grab your interest but the quality of each location varies.

Beachcombing

We did find some shells on this beach but only a couple worth taking home. If you spend some time really looking you might find a interesting specimen or two.

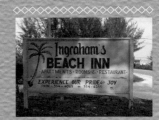

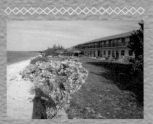

PRINCESS CAY MARKET

Tarpum Bay Beach

N 24° 58.570'~W 76° 10.602'

This miles-long, powdery coastline is the perfect example of a Caribbean beach. The water is calm, clear and turquoise. The sand is soft, white and firm enough for those long walks. And taking a long walk, or a short drive, to the northern end of the beach will bring you to a great shelling area. The sand is littered with all kinds of shells.

Directions to access road - heading south

19.5 miles (31.4 kms) south of **Duck Inn**. Turn right onto a sandy road. Look for the **Ingraham's Beach Inn** sign.

Directions to access road - heading north

0.0 miles (0.0 kms) The road to this beach is the road displaying the **Ingraham's Beach Inn** sign.

Leave the highway at N 24° 58.462'~W 76° 10.459'

and go just 0.2 miles (0.3 kms) to the beach. This is the **Ingraham's Beach Inn** driveway but restaurant guests are welcome to use the beach. If you're uncomfortable using this private access, continue north along the Queen's Highway for 2.8 miles (4.5 kms) to a short sandy road that goes to the shelling area of the beach as described above.

Access

The access road is short, sandy and a little bumpy in spots but nothing that any car would have difficulty with. Just keep an eye out for any dips and bumps, go slow and you'll be fine.

Privacy

Ingraham's Beach Inn is located directly on this beach, so you will have to share it with the hotel guests. But it's a very, very long beach, so you certainly won't feel crowded.

Swimming

As this in on the Caribbean side the water is calm and the bottom is even and sandy. This is a great place for a swim. But as we always mentioned, even the Caribbean side can get rough depending on the weather.

Snorkeling

In front of the hotel the sand is clean and smooth and not very interesting to the snorkeler. But go two miles up the beach and you will find some terrific snorkeling by the shelling site.

Beachcombing

We found lots and lots of shells at the north end of the beach, many intact and quite large. You could take home several nice specimens from this location.

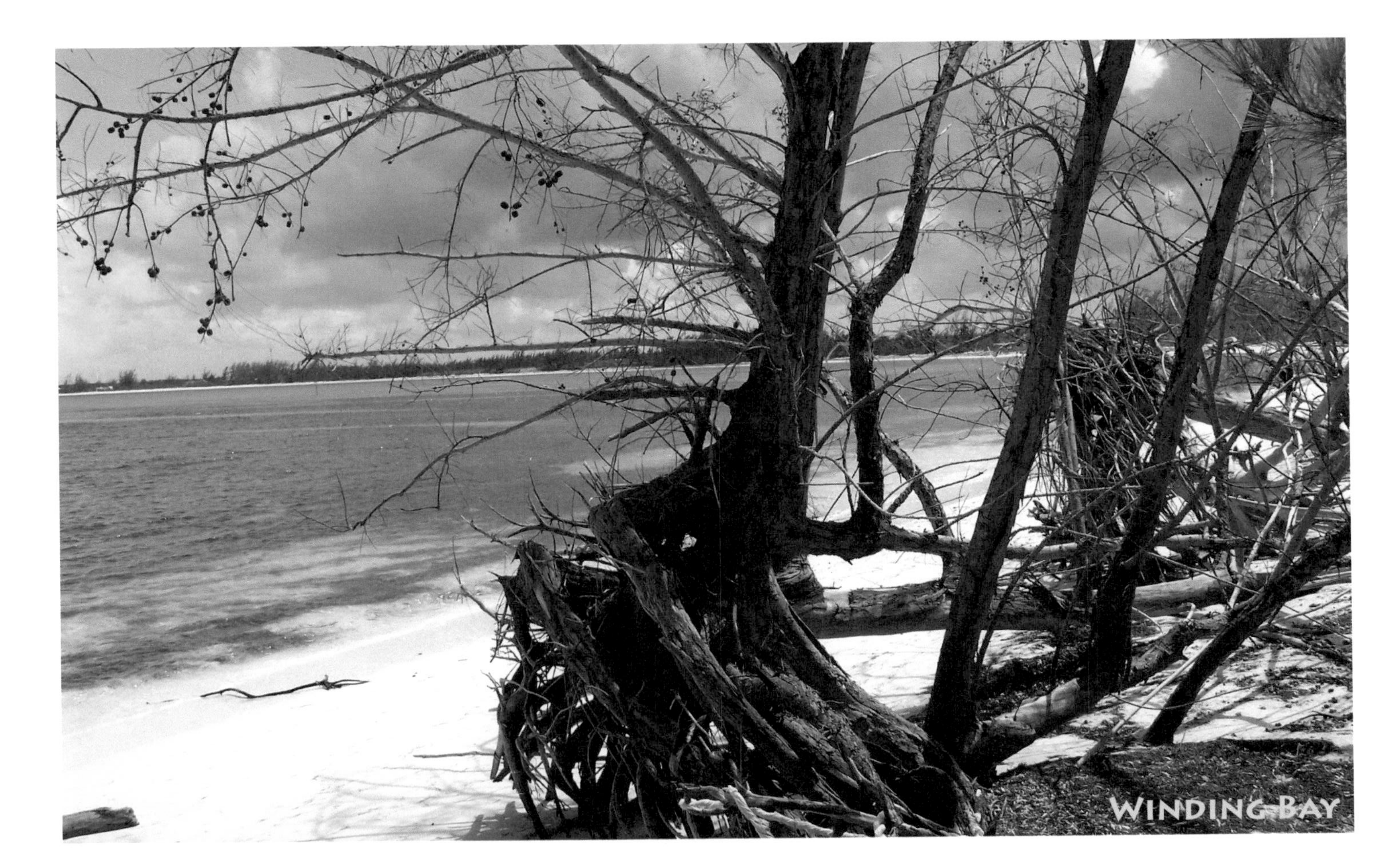
WINDING BAY

Winding Bay

N 24° 57.771'~W 76° 09.084'

REVISED: The beach at Winding Bay is long and curving and well protected from the Atlantic waves. The sand has a decidedly pink tinge to it. It's a lovely wide beach, but the sand can be a bit gravelly just as you enter the water. Other than that, well, it's just perfect. We have revised this listing because we discovered a better, more appealing access to this beach, which is also away from the homes that grace the opposite side of this bay. You can also continue on the access road and find Sand Quarry Beach - a new addition to this book.

Directions to access road - heading south

0.85 miles (1.3 kms) south of the **Signpost in Tarpum Bay**, turn left onto a paved road. Note: there is a Shell gas station on the corner.

Directions to access road - heading north

5.6 miles (9.0 kms) north of **Rock Sound Airport**, turn right onto a paved road. Note: there is a Shell gas station on the corner.

Leave the highway at N 24° 56.883'~W 76° 09.582'

and proceed for 1.4 miles (2.25 kms) to a sandy road on your left, just before the now closed Venta Club. Then proceed for another 1.2 miles (1.9 kms) to the sandy road on your right. Follow this sandy road a few hundred feet to the beach. The sand can get a bit loose, so park your car before getting all the way to the beach so you don't get stuck.

Access

There is paved road all the way to the road just before the now-closed Venta Club. It's a fairly good dirt and sand road the rest of the way. This access road can be negotiated by any car.

Privacy

Although The Venta Club is now closed, there are several private homes on the other end of this beach. The access we are showing is to the deserted end where you should find all the privacy you want. If you continue on to Sand Quarry beach (next page) you will have even more privacy.

Swimming

With this bay being reef protected, even though it is on the Atlantic side, the water stays fairly calm and shallow. You should be able to have a nice swimming experience here.

Snorkeling

It looks like there may be some snorkeling around the rocky areas at either end of the bay. We haven't tried it ourselves yet. It would certainly be worth giving it a try to see what might be lurking just beneath the surface.

Beachcombing

We didn't find many shells on this beach, but that's likely because the bay is reef protected. We did find some driftwood and some nets, though.

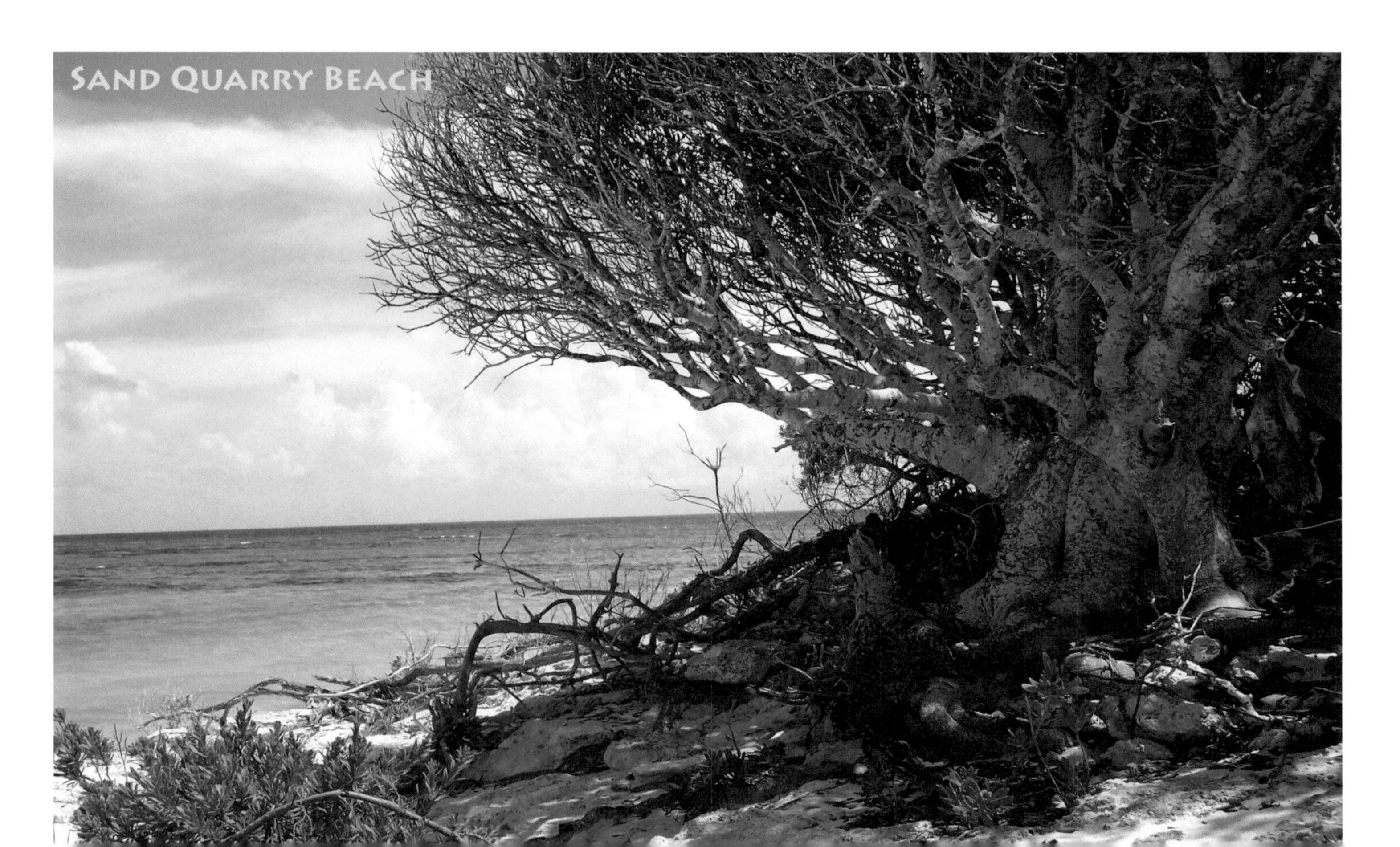
SAND QUARRY BEACH

Sand Quarry Beach

N24° 57.779' ~ W76° 08.841'

NEW: After visiting Winding Bay Beach, using the revised directions in this edition, you may want to continue on down the road until you get to the Sand Quarry and the Atlantic side beach that awaits just beyond the quarry. Park your car and continue to walk towards the Atlantic and you'll discover a lovely, wide, long Atlantic side beach. The sand is white and inviting and the water is typically deep Atlantic blue. We spent quite a bit of time here taking photos, soaking up the sunshine and walking along the beach listening to the waves hit the shore.

Directions to access road - heading south

0.85 miles (1.3 kms) south of the **Signpost in Tarpum Bay**, turn left onto a paved road. Note: there is a Shell gas station on the corner.

Directions to access road - heading north

5.6 miles (9.0 kms) north of **Rock Sound Airport**, turn right onto a paved road. Note: there is a Shell gas station on the corner.

Leave the highway at N 24° 56.883'~W 76° 09.582'

and proceed for 1.4 miles (2.25 kms) to a sandy road on your left, just before the now closed Venta Club. Then proceed for another 1.35 miles (2.2 kms) to the sand quarry. Find a safe place to park your car, out of the way of any heavy equipment that might be there, and walk the last little bit to the beach.

Access

The road is sandy with a few bumps and dips along the way, but is easily accessible by any vehicle. Be mindful that this is a quarry and stay out of the way of any equipment that might be there.

Privacy

This seems like a very private location, however, we found many, many footprints on this beach. So, we wouldn't expect it to be deserted all the time. It's obviously a great place for a long stroll beside the ocean.

Swimming

Just remember that you are on the Atlantic side. The water can get very rough and there is always the possibility of undertow, not to mention that it can become very deep, very quickly. Be sure to exercise caution if you plan to swim here.

Snorkeling

As mentioned above - remember that you are on the Atlantic side and give the ocean the respect it deserves. We have not tried snorkeling here, so we cannot give a recommendation, except to be careful if you try it here.

Beachcombing

As with most Atlantic side beaches, this beach gets its share of flotsam and jetsam. We actually came home from this beach with a fully inflated ring-type life preserver. There were some shells here, too, but most of them were well worn or broken.

CROWN POINT

N24° 56.269' ~ W76° 08.907'

NEW: At the very end of the road through the Coconut Forest, you'll find Crown Point, a cliff overlooking the entrance from the Atlantic into Half Sound. You'll get an impressive view from here and you can climb down, very carefully to get close to the water. We've taken several photographs from various angles and elevations. On your way to the point, you'll pass all the access points to the beach on the Atlantic side and the beach in Half Sound. Not to worry, you'll have a chance to stop at each one on your way out of the Coconut Forest.

Directions to access road - heading south

4.0 miles (6.4 kms) south of the **Signpost in Tarpum Bay**, turn left onto a paved, but broken, road. Keep your eyes on the mileage, as this road is easy to miss.

Directions to access road - heading north

2.45 miles (3.9 kms) north of **Rock Sound Airport**, turn right onto a paved, but broken, road. Keep your eyes on the mileage, as this road is easy to miss.

Leave the highway at N 24° 54.932'~W 76° 10.852'

and proceed for 4.0 miles (6.4 kms) to Crown Point. At 3.0 miles (4.8 kms) you'll come to a fork in the road - take the right fork. On the way out to Crown Point you'll pass a few clearings on your right. There is access to the Atlantic side beach from these points.

Access

From the Queen's Highway it is a mostly paved, if somewhat broken, road. However, you'll need to take it slow and easy through the Coconut Forest. There are lots of dips and bumps along this mostly sandy road. With care, any car can make it.

Privacy

As always, we found footprints on the beaches here. However, it's a long drive in and you need to be pretty determined to get all the way to Crown Point. Odds are, whenever you visit, you'll have the beaches all to yourselves.

Swimming

Remember that on the Atlantic side beaches the water can get pretty rough and the bottom can drop away rather dramatically. There's always the possibility of undertow as well. So, if you decide to swim here, please do so with caution.

Snorkeling

Again, the same admonition as for swimming here. Be mindful that you are on the Atlantic side. There are a few rocky outcroppings along the beach that may offer some interesting snorkeling.

Beachcombing

As with most Atlantic side beaches, this beach gets it share of interesting items washed ashore. We found nets, wood, what appeared to be a piece of the bow of a small boat and the usually assortment of shells.

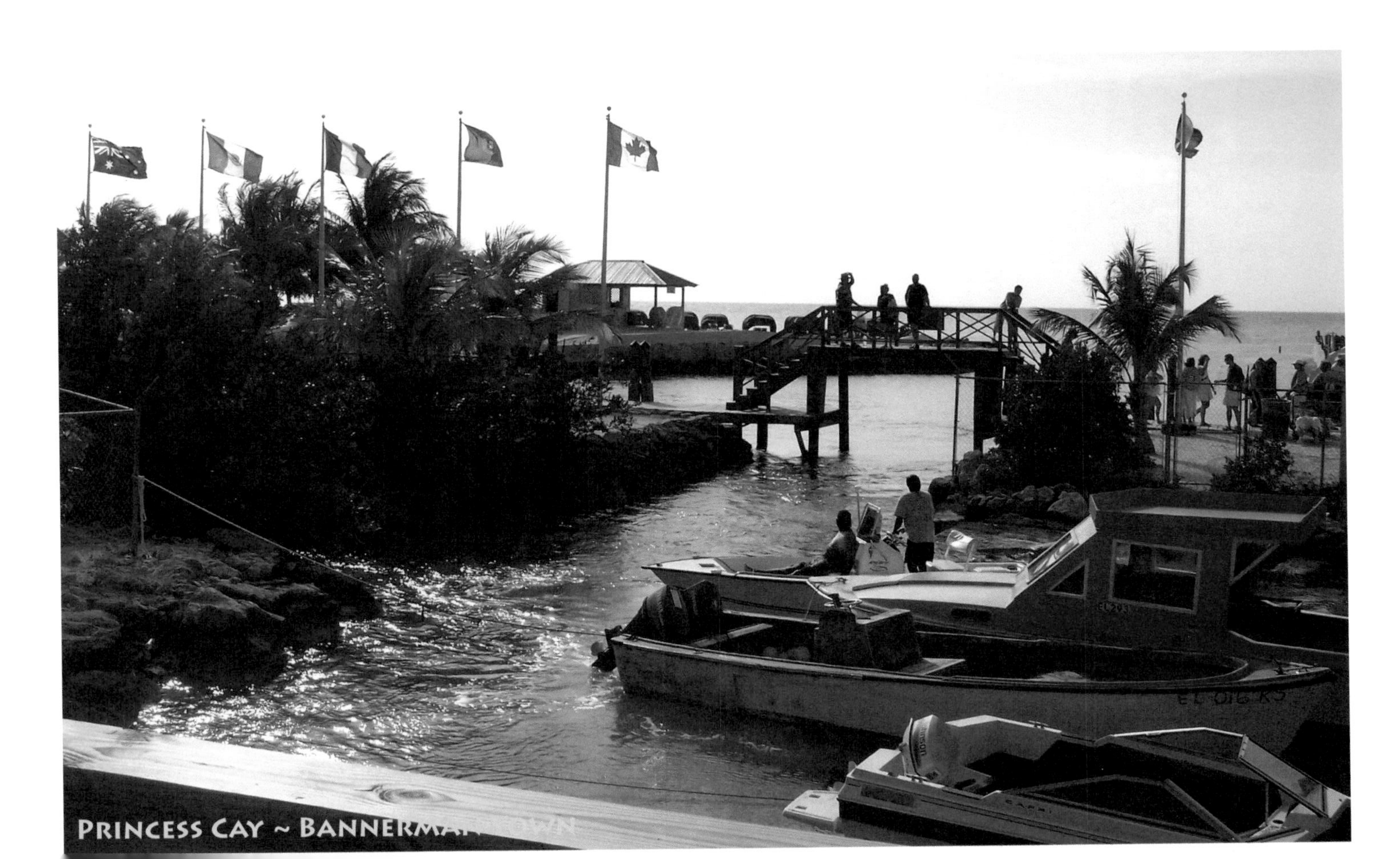

PRINCESS CAY ~ BANNERMAN TOWN

Half Sound Beach

N24° 56.983' ~ W76° 09.009'

NEW: While in the Coconut Forest, be sure to visit the beach at Half Sound as well. We're not sure we can actually call this an Atlantic side beach, even though it is, technically, on the Atlantic side of the island. But, as it is in a well-protected sound, the water is generally calm and shallow but the bottom can be a bit mushy in spots, particularly where there is vegetation growing. The beach is actually quite long and you can walk for a fair distance exploring towards Crown Point.

Directions to access road - heading south

4.0 miles (6.4 kms) south of the Signpost in Tarpum Bay, turn left onto a paved, but broken, road. Keep your eyes on the mileage, as this road is easy to miss.

Directions to access road - heading north

2.45 miles (3.9 kms) north of Rock Sound Airport, turn right onto a paved, but broken, road. Keep your eyes on the mileage, as this road is easy to miss.

Leave the highway at N 24° 54.932'~W 76° 10.852'

and proceed for 3.7 miles (5.95 kms) to the access road for Half Sound Beach. At 3.0 miles (4.8 kms) you'll come to a fork in the road - take the right fork. At 3.7 miles (5.95 kms) take the road on your left and proceed for .01 miles (0.16 kms) to the beach.

Access

It's a long way in from the Queen's Highway and sometimes it can seem pretty daunting, but if you're careful at the rougher spots pretty much any car can make it. However, if you have access to a four-wheel drive vehicle, that would be a better choice.

Privacy

We found footprints on this beach as well. However, it's a long drive in and you need to be pretty determined to find the road that leads to this Half Sound beach. Odds are you'll have the beach all to yourselves.

Swimming

The water in the Sound stays pretty calm and seems to be fairly shallow. There are a few mushy spots where you find vegetation in the water, so pick your swimming spot carefully and enjoy!

Snorkeling

We really need to have our snorkeling gear with us all the time, but, alas, we did not have it with us at this beach. You may, however, find some interesting fish hiding amongst the vegetation.

Beachcombing

This beach is so very well protected from the Atlantic waves that we just didn't find much here at all. We did find a few intact, but very small, shells. But, certainly, don't expect the variety of items that you will find on beaches that get the full force of Atlantic waves.

ROCK
SOUND
HARDWARE
THE
MARKET PLACE
The Market Place ~ Queen's Highway ~ Rock Sound
• Electronics • Major Appliances • Paint • Glass
P.O. Box 86, Rock Sound, Eleuthera
Phone: (242) 334-2253 Fax: (242) 334-2257

Ocean Hole

White Road Beach

N 24° 53.860'~W 76° 08.387'

This is another reef protected beach that is certainly worth stopping at for at least a look, if not a swim. The beach extends farther to the north than you can see from the access point. White Road Beach is a perfect spot for a long stroll on the beach, the sand is very firm near the shoreline making for easy walking. This is a beautiful, long, sandy beach much like Lighthouse beach (our personal favorite). With the easy access to this beach you have no excuse for not visiting this one during your explorations of Eleuthera.

Directions to access road - heading south

7.5 miles (12.0 kms) south of **Ingraham's Beach Inn**. Turn left at White Road. Watch for the road sign, it can be easy to miss.

Directions to access road - heading north

0.75 miles (1.2 kms) north of **Rock Sound Hardware.** Turn right at White Road. Watch for the road sign, it can be easy to miss.

Leave the highway at N 24° 53.055'~W 76° 09.711'

and proceed for 1.8 miles (2.9 kms) along White Road directly to the beach. It doesn't get much easier than that.

Access

A good portion of this access road is paved. With reasonable care the entire road is negotiable by any car right to the beach. Just be sure to watch for dips or bumps in the road.

Privacy

You may or may not be alone at this beach, so don't plan on a lot of privacy. We have run into other beachgoers while visiting this beach. We're sure other people like it as much as we do.

Swimming

Even though this beach is on the Atlantic side, it is good for swimming. There is a reef that protects this beach so the water is fairly calm and after an initial drop-off at the shoreline it stays fairly shallow for a long way out.

Snorkeling

There should be some good snorkeling around the rocky areas. We saw several playful fish even without our snorkel gear. Some of them followed us around through the water.

Beachcombing

There were a few shells on this beach. Keep your eyes open and you might spot some good ones.

Ocean Hole

N24° 51.838' ~ W76° 09.332'

Nope, this one isn't a beach either, but it deserves a place in this book nonetheless. The Ocean Hole is exactly that - an inland hole that is filled with ocean. There is obviously some subterranean connection to the sea that allows ocean fish to come and go. It is a popular attraction and you shouldn't miss it. You really can see many ocean fish - some quite large - and some very tame - right at the edge of the hole. Take a few slices of bread to feed them and they'll be your friends forever, or at least until the bread runs out. Don't forget to bring your camera to capture pictures of the unusual formation and of the feeding frenzy when you toss some tidbits to the eagerly awaiting schools of ocean fish. Sometimes people even bring their snorkeling or diving gear to the Ocean Hole.

Directions to access road - heading south

0.7 miles (1.1 kms) south of **Rock Sound Hardware** turn left at Fish Street. Watch for the street sign, it can be easy to miss.

Leave the highway at N 24° 51.825'~W 76° 09.552'

and proceed for 0.2 miles (0.3 kms) on Fish Street. Turn right at Ocean Hole sign and continue for another 0.06 miles (0.1 kms) to the parking area. Keep your eyes open for the street signs, they can be easy to miss.

Access

As the Ocean Hole is right in Rock Sound, there is a paved road all the way to the parking area. Any car can make it to this unique formation so you've got no reason to miss this one.

Privacy

This is a popular spot and, of course, not actually a beach, so you wouldn't expect any privacy here anyway. Also, there are frequently souvenir vendors showing their wares at the Ocean Hole.

Swimming

We've seen many of the local children swimming here and a pool ladder has been installed to make it easier to get out. If you're hot and sticky from a day of exploring we say go for it.

Snorkeling

It is said that Jacques Cousteau visited here and dove in The Ocean Hole. We believe is quite likely that he did as he also dove at Sweetings Pond. We haven't tried it ourselves but would like to one day.

Beachcombing

Like we said - it's not a beach.

North Side Beach Resort

N 24° 52.695'~W 76° 08.135'

The North Side Beach is a great place to stop and have lunch, or a drink, or just to relax. The resort boasts a unique, sand-floored bar and restaurant as well as three octagonal cottages all with a commanding view of both the ocean and the beach. The beach is soft, powdery and pink. There is easy access to the beach by a stairway from the bar. If you've just visited the Ocean Hole, then you're not far from this fabulous beach. So, there's no excuse not to take the time to come have a look, enjoy the beach and the ocean.

Directions to access road - heading south

0.7 miles (1.1 kms) south of **Rock Sound Hardware** turn left at Fish Street, which is also the road to Ocean Hole. Keep a good look out for the street sign because it can be easy to miss.

Leave the highway at N 24° 51.825'~W 76° 09.552'

and proceed for 1.5 miles (2.4 kms) on Fish Street. Fish Street is also the road to the Ocean Hole. Keep a look out for the street sign as it can be easy to miss. At the T-junction turn left for 0.5 miles (0.8 kms) and travel over a sandy road, with some dips, bump and hills, to **Northside Beach Bar and Resort**.

Access

All paved road except for the last half mile. With reasonable care this beach can be accessed by any car. Just be sure to watch out for the dips and bumps and be careful on the final sand hill up to the resort.

Privacy

With a hotel, bar and restaurant overlooking this location, don't expect any privacy. But don't let that stop you from visiting this fabulous beach and spending some quality time here.

Swimming

This is a good place to go swimming. The bottom is shallow and sandy. The water is relatively calm for the Atlantic side. But, if you plan to go swimming, be sure to pick a calm day.

Snorkeling

Try snorkeling around some of the rocky areas, but do it on a calm day. Remember that this is the Atlantic side and the waves can be pretty impressive depending on the weather conditions.

Beachcombing

We found a few shells at this beach but nothing compelling.

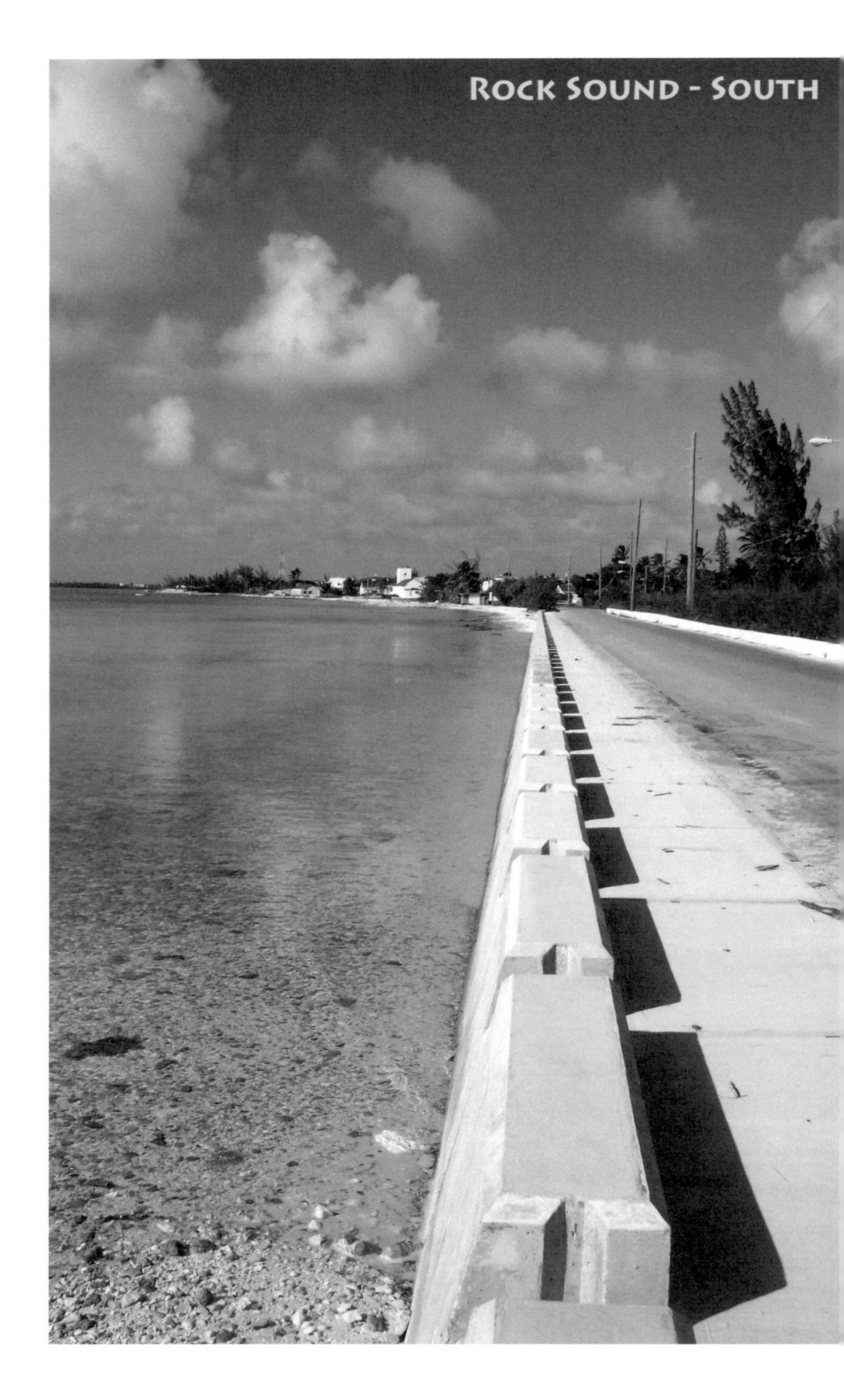
Rock Sound - South

North Side Beach Center

N 24° 52.210'~W 76° 08.081'

This small, shallow protected cove offers some privacy but it's just a stone's throw from the end of Fish Street, so don't plan on a lot of privacy. The sand is beige, soft and powdery. We wouldn't suggest a special trip for this beach, but if you're already in the area visiting the Ocean Hole, North Side Beach Resort or Whiteland Beach, then it's worth stopping by and having a look. There are several great beaches in this area. Take a look at North Side Beach Resort, North Side Beach South and Whiteland beach. They are all within an easy drive of this little piece of powdery soft sand lapped by warm, gentle ocean waves. Take the time to explore all of these beaches and you won't be disappointed.

Directions to access road - heading south

0.7 miles (1.1 kms) south of **Rock Sound Hardware** turn left at Fish Street, which is the road to Ocean Hole. Be sure to watch for the road sign because it can be easy to miss.

Leave the highway at N 24° 51.825'~W 76° 09.552'

and proceed for 1.5 miles (2.4 kms) on Fish Street. At the T-junction take the dirt road directly ahead of you for 0.2 miles (0.3 kms). It doesn't get much easier to find than that. It's right at the end of Fish Street.

Access

With reasonable care this beach can be accessed by any car. The road is paved a good part of the way and well-packed sand for the remainder. Just be sure to go slow and watch for dips and bumps in the road and you'll be fine.

Privacy

This small bay is relatively secluded and we found only a few footprints. However, it's just a few steps from the bottom of Fish Street at the junction to find the other beaches mentioned above. Don't expect any privacy here.

Swimming

This small protected cove offers a good swimming opportunity. The bottom is sandy and even and there was little undertow. But, as we always caution, as this is the Atlantic side, swim on a calm day.

Snorkeling

Try snorkeling around the rocky areas, but best to do it on a calm day. Although the water is calm here a lot of the time, some good-sized waves can still kick up in this little cove.

Beachcombing

We didn't find many good specimens at this beach, but keep your eyes open - you never know.

Eleuthera Clinics

Settlement	*Phone No.*
Harbour Island	333-3417 333-2227
Spanish Wells	333-4087 333-4064 333-5168
Hatchet Bay / Alice Town	335-0091 335-0669
James Cistern	335-6333
Bluff	335-1122
Gregory Town	335-5108
Lower Bogue	335-1089
Governor's Harbour	332-2774
Palmetto Point	335-1520
Savannah Sound	332-6027
Rock Sound	334-2226
Tarpum Bay	334-4102
Greencastle	334-6419
Wemyss Bight	334-0077

Not every clinic is open every day. If you plan to visit one of the clinics, it's a good idea to call ahead. When a clinic is open there is a practical nurse on duty. Doctors travel from clinic to clinic on specific days. If you require a doctor, call the clinic to find out which day the doctor will be in.

N 24° 51.947'~W 76° 08.104'

The other two beaches making up Northside Beach are better than this small sandy cove, but this one is worth a look for shelling and snorkeling. This may be a popular spot for some of the local fishermen, as we found a boat beached here. We don't believe that there is any such thing as a bad beach, not in Eleuthera anyway. However, this one is not top of our list. But, as we mentioned in the previous pages, this is a terrific area in which to visit several beaches, some good, some great and some absolutely fabulous. All of the beaches in this area are worth visiting but you'll want to spend more time at some and less time at others. But finding each of these beaches is an adventure worth pursuing.

Directions to access road - heading south

0.7 miles (1.1 kms) south of **Rock Sound Hardware** turn left at Fish Street, which is the road to Ocean Hole. Be sure to watch for the sign for Fish Street, it can be easy to miss.

Leave the highway at N 24° 51.825'~W 76° 09.552'

and proceed for 1.5 miles (2.4 kms) on Fish Street. Be sure to watch for the sign for Fish Street, it can be easy to miss. Turn right at the T-junction and go another 0.5 miles (0.8 kms) and take the first left.

Access

With reasonable care this beach can be accessed by any car. The road is paved a good part of the way and well-packed sand for the remainder. Just keep your eyes open for dips and bumps in the road and drive slowly.

Privacy

We have never seen anyone but there are lots of footprints and a there was a boat on this beach, so don't expect much privacy. We suspect it may be a spot frequented by local fishermen.

Swimming

This beach is in a small protected cove and offers some good swimming. The bottom is clean and sandy. And, as we always caution, if you're going to swim here, do it on a calm day.

Snorkeling

We found some conch shells on this beach so you may want to try some snorkeling here. Always check the weather and pick a calm day to snorkel as well as swim. The Atlantic waves can often get rough.

Beachcombing

Along with some conch shells there were other types of shells as well. You might want to spend some time looking around.

Eleuthera Banks

Name	*Settlement*	*Phone No.*	*Days/Hours*	*ATM*
First Caribbean (formerly Barclays)	Governor's Harbour	332-2300 332-2303	Monday - Thursday 9:30 am to 3:00 pm Friday 9:30 am to 4:30 pm	Yes
Royal Bank of Canada	Governor's Harbour	332-2856 332-2857 332-2858 332-2526 (fax)	Monday - Thursday 9:30 am to 3:00 pm Friday 9:30 am to 4:30 pm	Yes
Royal Bank of Canada	Spanish Wells	333-4131 333-4145 333-4648 (fax)	Monday 9:00 am - 3:00 pm Tuesday - Thursday 9:30 am to 1:00 pm Friday 9:30 am - 4:30 pm	Yes
Royal Bank of Canada	Harbour Island	333-2250 333-2270 333-2280 (fax)	Monday - Thursday 9:30 am to 3:00 pm Friday 9:30 am to 4:30 pm	Yes
Scotiabank	North Eleuthera (near airport)	335-1400 335-1401 335-1402 335-1403 335-1399 (fax)	Monday - Thursday 9:30 am to 3:00 pm Friday 9:30 am to 4:30 pm **Note**: can replace lost traveler's checks	Yes
Scotiabank	Rock Sound	334-2620 334-2621 334-2622 334-2623 334-2619 (fax)	Monday - Thursday 9:30 am to 3:00 pm Friday 9:30 am to 4:30 pm	Yes

Whiteland Beach

N 24° 49.979'~W 76° 08.690'

It seems that the more difficult a beach is to find, the more spectacular it is - and Whiteland Beach is no exception. The shore is lined with palm trees. The sand is white and powdery soft. The water is turquoise, warm and welcoming. At the end of the access road you come upon a tiny cove and the rest of the beach stretches out on either side of this cove. Be sure to bring your camera with you to this beach. It is truly like something out of a South Pacific movie or, at the very least, a perfect picture postcard setting. We have picked this as one of our ten favorite beaches in Eleuthera and when you visit Whiteland Beach you will understand why we have put this one on such a prestigious list.

Directions to access road - heading south

0.7 miles (1.1 kms) south of **Rock Sound Hardware**, turn left onto Fish Street. Keep you eyes open for this Fish Street sign, it can be easy to miss.

Leave the highway at N 24° 51.825'~W 76° 09.552'

and continue for 1.5 miles (2.4 kms) along Fish Street until you reach a T-junction. Turn right and continue for 2.9 miles (4.7 kms). The road veers to the left as you are nearing the beach area. Just before the beach the road takes a sharp 90 deg bend to the left.

Access

Access is by some paved road and some packed sand roads. With only a few bumpy areas, this mostly sandy road can be handled by any car. Just go slowly and keep your eyes open for the dips and bumps.

Privacy

There were a few footprints on this beach but it is rather out of the way. It's not a place a regular tourist would be able to find without directions. You may or may not have some privacy here.

Swimming

The area is reef protected and has an even, sandy bottom. With this expanse of beach you could spend a lot of time swimming here. As this is the Atlantic side, be sure to swim on a calm day.

Snorkeling

Bring your snorkel gear along and investigate the rocky areas and the coral heads out in the water. And, as we always caution, snorkel on a calm day. Atlantic side waves can get pretty impressive at times.

Beachcombing

We found a few shells here but nothing of consequence. But, don't let that stop you from visiting this exceptional beach.

Eleuthera Gas Stations

Name	*Settlement*	*Phone No.*	*Diesel*
North Eleuthera Texaco	Airport Corner, Lower Bogue	242-335-1548 or 242-335-1128	Yes
Rollin Service Station	Gregory Town	242-335-5550	Yes
Gateway Service Station & Car Rental	Hatchet Bay	242-335-0455	Coming soon
D&D Service Station	James Cistern	242-335-6444	•
Culmers Balara Bay Esso	N of Governor's Harbour	242-332-3255	Yes
Eleuthera Supply Shell	Governor's Harbour	242-332-2728	•
Highway Esso	Governor's Harbour	242-332-2077	Yes
CS Service Station & Mini Mart	Palmetto Point	242-332-0033	•
Sands Enterprises	Palmetto Point	242-332-1662	No
Savannah Sound Gas Station	Savannah Sound		•
Buy Wise Gas Station	Tarpum Bay	242-334-4180	•
Kinky's Korner Shell Station	Tarpum Bay	242-334-4208	•
Market Place Shell	Rock Sound		•
Carey's Service Station	Rock Sound	242-334-2165	•
Kell's Service Station	Wemyss Bight	242-334-0104	•

This is not a complete list of all the gas stations on the island but it is fairly close. The message here is if you need gas, get it when you can and don't wait until the tank is almost empty. If you are used to gas stations on every corner that are open 24 hours a day you will need to adjust to the island way of doing things. And don't forget - most will be closed on Sundays.

Jack's Bay

N 24° 47.093'~W 76° 10.381'

This beach rivals the beauty of Lighthouse beach even if it doesn't rival the size. This reasonably large bay is reef protected and, therefore, remains calm and clean most of the time. The sand is soft, powdery and pink and is firm enough to make walking the shoreline both pleasant and easy. Jack's Bay is definitely worth the effort to find. It is also on our list of the ten best beaches in Eleuthera. Bring your camera to this beach as well and try taking pictures from several perspectives here. On sunny days the turquoise of the ocean complements the pink of the sand. With the palm trees and other vegetation as a backdrop the scene is - well, for lack of any better words - picture perfect!

Directions to access road - heading south

7.3 miles (11.8 kms) south of **Rock Sound Hardware** turn left at the road with Cotton Bay Club signs on either side. Keep your eyes open for these signs, they're not very big.

Leave the highway at N 24° 46.806'~W 76° 11.605'

and proceed for 0.75 miles (1.2 kms) and turn left onto a dirt road. Take the dirt road for 1.8 miles (3.0 kms). The access to the beach is the first road on your right past the two houses.

Access

The paved road that takes you part way has several potholes. The dirt road that takes you the rest of the way can be a bit bumpy but any car can make it. Just keep your eyes open for the potholes, dips and bumps and you'll be fine.

Privacy

We were tempted to give this beach a high rating for privacy, but there are two houses on the beach. It is a fairly large bay and we didn't encounter anyone else on the beach while we were there, but there are usually footprints in the sand.

Swimming

This reef protected bay is perfect for swimming. As always, though, pick a calm day for swimming on the Atlantic side. The reef does dampen most of the waves, but some can still get through when it's rough.

Snorkeling

The rocky areas and overhanging cliffs at each end of the bay offer some terrific snorkeling. Again, always do your snorkeling on calm days so you can be sure to enjoy the experience.

Beachcombing

We couldn't find much in the way of shells at all at this beach. We suspect the reef filters out a lot.

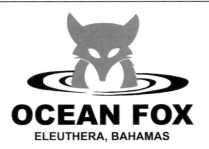

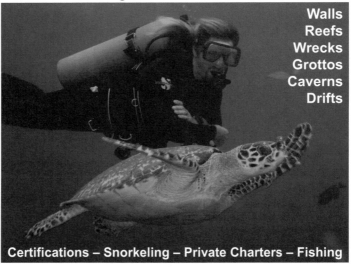

Cotton Bay Beach

N 24° 45.158'~W 76° 11.607'

Unfortunately, the Cotton Bay Club has been closed since 1994. Even still, this beach is definitely worth taking the time to the visit. The gently curving bay is reef protected so the warm and welcoming crystal clear water stays calm most of the time and the powdery pink sand stays relatively clean of any of the flotsam that can wash ashore on a lot of the Atlantic beaches. Cotton Bay Beach is not far from Jack's Bay, so, if you are pressed for time while on the island, you could plan to visit both of these beaches on the same day.

Directions to access road - heading south

7.3 miles (11.8 kms) south of **Rock Sound Hardware** turn left at the road with Cotton Bay Club signs on either side. Keep your eyes open for these signs. They're not very big and are easily missed.

Leave the highway at N 24° 46.806'~W 76° 11.605'

and proceed for 2.0 miles (3.3 kms) to the Cotton Bay Club entrance (look for the sign and white picket fence). Turn left into the club entrance and then right at the first dirt road - 0.2 miles (0.3 kms) from the entrance. There is usually security at the entrance to the club, even though it is closed. However, they directed us to the road we mention here for access to the beach.

Access

There are a few potholes at the beginning of the paved access road but it's good road right to the beach. Just take it slow and watch for the potholes and you'll get there in one piece.

Privacy

As the Cotton Bay Club is currently closed, you can expect more privacy than you would with the resort open. It still gets some traffic and there are security guards on duty.

Swimming

The water is calm with little undertow in this reef protected bay. As we always caution, be sure to swim on a calm day. The waves can still get pretty impressive from time to time.

Snorkeling

Check out the rocky areas for some ho-hum snorkeling. We didn't see much, but it was still pleasant just being in the water and floating around looking for whatever sea creatures were obviously trying to hide from us.

Beachcombing

It doesn't look like many shells get past the reef. We certainly didn't find any.

Ten Best Beaches of Eleuthera

Lighthouse Beach

N 24° 37.006'~W 76° 08.750'

REVISED: Lighthouse Beach is our favorite beach on Eleuthera. A 3 mile long, wide, pink sand beach that wraps itself around the southern tip of the island. On certain days you can watch as cruise ships go by either on their way to or from Princess Cay. Come early and plan to spend the day. You can find some shade amongst the cliffs at the southern end of the beach. As this beach wraps right around the tip, you'll pass by a part of it on the Caribbean side as you make your way to the main beach. You can also stop at the northerly part of the beach. After you leave the Queen's Highway, you'll pass a road on your left at 1.0 miles (1.6 kms). This is an overgrown road, so your car will likely get scratched, but follow it for 0.5 miles (0.8 kms) and you'll find access to the northern section of the beach. It looks like you may be able to walk all the way from here to the tip of Lighthouse beach. It would take a while but make an interesting day.

Directions to access road - heading south

18.1 miles (29.2 kms) south of **Rock Sound Hardware,** at the "Welcome to Bannerman Town" sign, the highway takes a 90 degree bend to the right. The access road goes straight through.

Leave the highway at N 24° 39.166'~W 76° 10.168'

and proceed on a paved/coral road for 3.3 miles (5.35 kms). At 3.2 miles (5.2 kms) you'll pass the Caribbean section on your right and the road takes a sharp bend to the left going over some sand dunes. Without 4 wheel drive you may want to park here.

Access

An SUV is preferable but a regular sedan can make it if you're very, very careful over a couple of rough spots. We recommend an SUV for the clearance it would give you over some of the rougher spots on the road.

Privacy

Even though this huge beach is, without a doubt, the best in Eleuthera it is rare to find many other people here. That would, of course, depend on the time of year you come here, but it will certainly never be crowded.

Swimming

Even though this beach is on the Atlantic side it is calm and shallow with little undertow. Just keep an eye to the weather, though, as it is possible to be some rough waves here.

Snorkeling

Snorkeling around the rocks could bring unexpected pleasures. We sighted a manta ray on one of our trips. We were also joined by some playful fish that wanted to swim with us while we were snorkeling.

Beachcombing

We didn't find a lot of shells here, but keep your eyes open - you never know.

	Wemyss Bight	Waterford	Upper Bogue	Tarpum Bay	Spanish Wells Dock	Savannah Sound	Rock Sound Airport RSD	Rock Sound	Rainbow Subdivision	Palmetto Point	N. Eleuthera Airport ELH	Lower Bogue	John Millars	James Cistern	Hatchet Bay	Harbour Island Dock	Gregory Town	Greencastle	Gov. Harbour Airport GBH	Governor's Harbour	Glass Window Bridge	Deep Creek	Current	Cape Eleuthera	Bluff	Bannerman Town
Bannerman Town	6	7	74	25	84	34	19	18	62	40	80	78	4	52	60	80	66	8	53	45	70	13	83	17	79	••
Bluff	75	74	7	56	7	47	62	63	23	46	5	3	77	29	21	6	15	71	49	41	11	80	10	84	••	79
Cape Eleuthera	11	10	77	28	87	37	22	21	65	43	83	81	14	55	63	83	69	12	56	48	73	4	86	••	84	17
Current	77	76	9	58	12	49	64	65	25	48	9	5	79	31	23	8	17	73	35	43	13	82	••	86	10	83
Deep Creek	7	6	73	24	83	33	18	17	61	39	78	87	11	51	59	79	65	8	52	44	69	••	82	4	80	13
Glass Window Bridge	64	63	4	45	14	36	51	52	12	35	10	8	66	18	10	10	4	60	22	30	••	82	13	73	4	81
Governor's Harbour	39	38	24	20	44	11	26	27	17	5	39	38	41	12	20	34	25	36	8	••	30	69	43	48	41	45
Gov. Harbour Airport GBH	46	45	26	28	36	19	34	35	9	13	31	30	48	4	12	26	17	42	••	8	22	51	35	55	49	50
Greencastle	3	2	64	15	74	24	10	9	52	30	69	78	6	42	50	70	56	••	43	35	60	8	73	13	71	8
Gregory Town	60	59	8	41	18	32	47	48	8	31	13	12	62	14	6	14	••	56	18	26	4	65	17	69	15	64
Harbour Island Dock	74	73	6	55	9	46	61	62	22	45	1	18	76	28	20	••	14	70	32	40	10	79	8	83	6	78
Hatchet Bay	54	53	14	35	24	26	41	42	2	25	19	18	56	8	••	20	5	50	12	20	10	59	23	63	21	58
James Cistern	46	45	22	27	32	18	33	34	6	17	27	26	48	••	8	28	13	42	4	12	18	51	31	55	29	50
John Millars	4	5	70	21	80	30	15	14	58	36	75	84	••	48	56	76	62	6	49	41	66	11	79	15	77	4
Lower Bogue	82	81	4	53	7	44	69	70	16	43	2	••	84	26	18	3	12	78	30	38	8	87	5	91	3	86
N. Eleuthera Airport ELH	73	72	6	54	8	45	60	61	21	44	••	2	75	27	19	1	13	69	31	39	10	78	9	83	5	80
Palmetto Point	34	33	39	15	49	6	21	22	22	••	21	48	36	16	24	45	29	30	13	21	35	39	48	43	46	38
Rainbow Subdivision	56	55	16	37	26	28	43	44	••	22	44	16	58	6	2	22	8	52	9	17	12	61	25	65	23	60
Rock Sound	16	11	56	7	66	16	1	••	44	22	61	70	14	34	42	62	48	8	35	27	52	17	65	21	63	16
Rock Sound Airport RSD	17	12	55	6	65	15	••	1	43	21	60	69	15	33	41	61	47	9	34	26	51	18	64	22	62	17
Savannah Sound	28	27	40	9	50	••	15	16	28	6	45	44	30	18	26	46	32	24	19	11	36	33	49	37	47	32
Spanish Wells Dock	78	77	10	59	••	50	65	66	26	49	8	7	80	32	24	9	18	74	36	44	14	83	12	87	7	82
Tarpum Bay	19	18	49	••	59	9	6	7	37	15	54	53	21	27	35	55	41	15	28	20	45	24	58	28	56	23
Upper Bogue	68	67	••	49	10	40	55	56	16	39	6	4	70	22	14	6	8	64	26	34	4	73	9	77	7	72
Waterford	1	••	67	18	77	27	12	11	55	33	72	81	5	45	53	73	59	2	46	38	63	6	76	10	74	7
Wemyss Bight	••	1	68	19	78	28	13	12	56	34	73	82	4	46	54	74	60	3	47	39	64	7	77	11	75	6

Made in United States
Troutdale, OR
02/02/2024